A Primer on Policies for Jobs

A Primer on Policies for Jobs

Raj Nallari, Breda Griffith, Yidan Wang, Soamiely Andriamananjara, Derek H. C. Chen, and Rwitwika Bhattacharya

THE WORLD BANK
Washington, D.C.

1 2 3 4 14 13 12 11

This volume is a product of the staff of The World Bank with external contributions. The findings, interpretations, and conclusions expressed in this volume do not necessarily reflect the views of The World Bank, its Board of Executive Directors, or the governments they represent.

The World Bank does not guarantee the accuracy of the data included in this work. The boundaries, colors, denominations, and other information shown on any map in this work do not imply any judgment on the part of The World Bank concerning the legal status of any territory or the endorsement or acceptance of such boundaries.

ISBN (paper): 978-0-8213-8904-1
ISBN (electronic): 978-0-8213-8905-8
DOI: 10.1596/978-0-8213-8904-1

Library of Congress Cataloging-in-Publication Data
A primer on policies for jobs / Raj Nallari ... [et al.].
    p. cm.
Includes bibliographical references and index.
  ISBN 978-0-8213-8904-1 — ISBN 978-0-8213-8905-8 (electronic)
  1. Labor market. 2. Manpower policy. 3. Entrepreneurship. 4. Economic development.
I. Nallari, Raj, 1955-
  HD5706.P735 2011
  331.12'042—dc23

2011032973

Cover photo: Worker in factory, India. Ray Witlin/World Bank
Cover design: Quantum Think

Contents

Tables

Preface

A Primer on Policies for Jobs is based on materials and input provided during the labor market courses conducted during the past 10 years. Its objective is to provide government policy makers, researchers, and labor market practitioners and other specialists with a practical guide on how to strengthen labor market institutions, especially in light of the global financial crisis. This primer emphasizes six pillars of labor market institutions: global trends, job creation, labor market policies, education, entrepreneurship, and globalization.

Chapter 1 addresses current labor market trends and job creation, particularly in tough conditions. **Chapter 2** examines channels of job creation and ways to strengthen labor market institutions to ensure sustainable job growth, considering factors such as investment climate, job policy, industrial policy, social protection, and other labor market issues. **Chapter 3** focuses on labor market policies in developing countries. Following a brief introduction about the MILES Framework, the chapter examines the degree of informal employment in labor markets in developing countries. This analysis provides a context for the subsequent discussion of labor market policies in developing economies. The discussion focuses on the issues in job to worker protection. **Chapter 4** highlights the impact of education and skills on labor market outcome, particularly in the developing world. **Chapter 5** discusses entrepreneurship along three key dimensions: development and growth, job creation, and female entrepreneurship. It first discusses the importance of entrepreneurship in economic development and consequently job creation and then shifts to the topic of gender differences in entrepreneurship. Finally, **chapter 6** addresses the relationship between jobs and globalization. As trade and services across borders continue to grow, globalization has had a tremendous influence on the labor market.

The authors would like to thank participants in the labor market course for their input and to acknowledge the International Labour Organization for its valuable data.

About the Authors

Raj Nallari is the sector manager for the Growth and Competitiveness Practice at the World Bank Institute (WBI). He has worked at the World Bank for more than 20 years in various departments. Previously, he worked at the International Monetary Fund. He has published on various topics, including growth adjustment systems, the labor market and gender, and macroeconomics. He has also edited several volumes of development outreach. He holds a PhD in economics from the University of Texas at Austin.

Breda Griffith holds a PhD in economics from Trinity College Dublin and a master's degree in economics from the National University of Ireland. She has worked as a consultant with WBI since 2005 in the areas of growth, poverty, gender, development, and labor markets. Her experience is deep and wide-ranging, with publications in refereed journals on development and language maintenance, entrepreneurship, and small business. She has also coauthored books on economic growth, poverty, gender and macroeconomic policy, new directions in development, and labor markets in developing countries.

Yidan Wang is a senior education specialist at WBI, where she has been developing new core courses, including "Transforming Tertiary Education for Innovation and Competitiveness," "Education for Development and Competitiveness," "Challenges and Opportunities for Post-Basic Education," "Public-Private Partnerships in Secondary Education," and others. Previously, she worked for the Asian Development Bank. Her publications include *Public-Private Partnerships in the Social Sector, The China Experience: Providing Teacher Training through Educational Television,* and *Expanding Opportunities and Building Competencies for Young People: A New Agenda for Secondary Education.* She has held several academic positions, including professor, visiting professor, and visiting scholar at the State University of New York and Harvard University in the United States, and Peking University and Northeast Normal University in China. Wang holds a doctorate from the University of Pittsburgh.

Soamiely Andriamananjara is a senior economist at the WBI and works on trade policy issues. Previously, he was an international economist in the research division of the U.S. International Trade Commission, where he conducted quantitative and qualitative studies on various trade-related topics. Recently, he published academic and policy research papers on regional integration, textiles and clothing quotas, international transport services, and nontariff trade barriers. He holds a PhD in economics from the University of Maryland at College Park, with a concentration in international economics.

Derek H. C. Chen is an economist with the World Bank, which he joined in 2000, after receiving his doctoral degree in economics from the University of California, Davis. His specializations include economic growth, international economics, poverty analysis, and demographic economics. He leads WBI's program on employment policies. Chen has written on topics relating to economic growth and knowledge accumulation. Previously, he taught undergraduate economics at the University of California, Davis and at the National University of Singapore.

Rwitwika Bhattacharya is a junior professional associate at the World Bank. She holds a master's degree in public policy with a concentration in business and government from the Harvard Kennedy School. She has written Harvard Business School cases. Previously, she worked for the United Nations Population Fund.

Abbreviations

ALMP	active labor market policy
CIS	Commonwealth of Independent States
EPL	employment protection legislation
EU	European Union
FDI	foreign direct investment
GDP	gross domestic product
GEM	Global Entrepreneurship Monitor
GTZ	German Agency for Technical Cooperation (Deutsche Gesellschaft für Technische Zusammenarbeit)
ICT	information and communication technology
IDB	Inter-American Development Bank
ILO	International Labour Organization
IMF	International Monetary Fund
IZA	Institute for the Study of Labor
MDG	Millennium Development Goal
MENA	Middle East and North Africa (World Bank region)
MILES	(framework) macroeconomic performance, investment climate, labor market policies and institutions, education and skills, and social protection for workers
PW	public works

R&D	research and development
SIC	Standard Industrial Classification
TEA	total entrepreneurial activity
UA	unemployment assistance
UI	unemployment insurance
UISA	unemployment insurance savings account
WBI	World Bank Institute
WDR	*World Development Report*
WEF	World Economic Forum
WP	work program

CHAPTER 1

The Global Labor Market: Trends and Outcomes

The chapter examines the labor market, incorporating the available information to inform on the global labor market situation, particularly in the aftermath of the global financial crisis. The labor market is discussed within the context of the macroeconomic environment, highlighting the uneven global economic recovery and the delayed revival of the labor market. Stubbornly high levels of unemployment stand in contrast to the upturn witnessed in many macroeconomic indicators.

Other key indicators of the labor market are discussed, including employment, labor force participation, vulnerable employment, working poverty, and gender disparity. Labor markets are very different in the developing world from those in the developed countries. The majority of workers in developing regions are employed in the informal economy and face disadvantaged working conditions. Inadequate or nonexistent social protection in developing economies means that workers have little choice but to offer their services often as unpaid family workers in agriculture. Labor is the main asset of the poor, and finding a job is the main way out of poverty.

The regions of the world, developing and advanced, face key challenges in their labor markets. A wide array of factors affects labor market outcomes, including labor market conditions, natural resources, and cultural factors. Globalization and technological change also affect labor market outcomes.

The *2011 Global Employment Trends* from the International Labour Organization (ILO) takes stock of the labor market in the developed and developing economies. This chapter draws heavily on its findings for the discussion of the global labor market situation in the sections that follow.

The Global Economic Recovery and the Labor Market

The financial crisis that rocked the global economy from late 2007 through early 2009 adversely affected unemployment and employment. Three years later, as the world economy begins to recover,[1] the gains in output (see table 1.1) have not been matched by decreases in unemployment. The number of unemployed in 2010—some 205 million—was unchanged from a year earlier and above the level that prevailed before the crisis, approximately 177.4 million in 2007. A marginal improvement in the global unemployment rate—6.2 percent in 2010 as opposed to 6.3 percent in 2009—was far from the 5.6 percent prevailing in 2007. The vigorous pursuit of countercyclical fiscal and monetary policies is credited with halting the crisis and bringing about a recovery in growth that occurred faster than was forecast. Global growth began to recover in the final quarter of 2009 (ILO 2011, 4) and was estimated at 4.8 percent in 2010 with a (projected) deceleration to 4.2 percent in 2011 (see table 1.1). The current global economic environment—characterized by fragile labor markets, high levels of public and household debt, and continuing vulnerabilities in the financial sector—constitutes significant downside risks to growth in the near term (ILO 2011, 4).

The pace of recovery has been unequal, with developing economies having rebounded faster than the developed countries. The crisis began in the developed economies, and the fiscal and monetary policy responses have generated unsustainable government debt that acts as a brake on economic growth. In contrast, the rapid recovery in global trade has generated a faster than expected recovery in the developing economies and the emerging markets in particular. Moreover, returns on capital have been greatest in emerging economies, and they have experienced large increases in capital flows. While there are downside risks—asset bubbles and inflation—in the short term the emerging economies have rebounded faster.

Furthermore, employment generation has been slow in developed economies, and developing economies have seen an increase in employment

Table 1.1   Real Annual Growth of Gross Domestic Product by Region, 2005–11
(percent)

Region	2005	2006	2007	2008	2009	2010	2011
World	4.6	5.2	5.3	2.8	−0.6	4.8	4.2
Developed economies and European Union	2.6	2.9	2.6	0.3	−3.4	2.3	2.0
Central and south-eastern Europe (non-EU) and CIS	7.0	8.2	7.9	4.3	−6.0	4.9	4.3
East Asia	9.5	10.8	12.1	7.8	7.0	9.8	8.6
Latin America and the Caribbean	4.7	5.6	5.7	4.3	−1.7	5.7	4.0
Middle East	5.4	5.6	6.1	4.8	1.3	3.6	5.1
North Africa	5.0	6.1	5.8	5.3	3.5	5.1	5.1
South Asia	8.7	9.0	9.1	5.9	5.5	8.9	7.7
Southeast Asia and the Pacific	5.9	6.2	6.7	4.4	1.5	7.2	5.3
Sub-Saharan Africa	6.3	6.4	6.9	5.5	2.6	5.0	5.5

Source: ILO 2011, 61.
Note: Estimates for 2010 and 2011 are preliminary.

in the informal sector and among the working poor. The failure of employment growth to keep pace with improvements in macroeconomic indicators provides a real challenge to the labor market and to future sustainable growth of the macroeconomy. Distress in a number of labor market indicators—employment-to-population ratio, vulnerable employment, and working poor—highlights the challenges the labor market is facing.

The employment-to-population ratio—the share of the working-age population that is employed—is an indicator of whether a country is generating employment. The global employment-to-population ratio, as shown in table 1.2, has fallen since the crisis and was estimated to fall further in 2010, suggesting that the global economy is not generating sufficient employment. Across the regions, the ratio is estimated to increase (improve) for all regions except East Asia, Southeast Asia, and the Pacific and to stay the same for Sub-Saharan Africa (see table 1.2).

Vulnerable employment refers to family workers and own-account workers and is a measure of informal sector employment. South Asia and Sub-Saharan Africa show the highest rate of vulnerable workers, reflecting the significant numbers employed in the agricultural sector. Before the crisis, the share of vulnerable workers was declining across all regions (see table 1.3). Between 2008 and 2009, the rate of vulnerable

Table 1.2 Employment-to-Population Ratio by Region, 2000–10
(percent)

Both sexes	2000	2004	2005	2006	2007	2008	2009	2010 CI lower bound	2010 Preliminary estimate	2010 CI upper bound
World	61.5	61.4	61.4	61.6	61.7	61.6	61.2	60.9	61.1	61.3
Developed economies and European Union	56.7	55.9	56.2	56.7	57.1	57.1	55.5	54.5	54.7	54.9
Central and southeastern Europe (non-EU) and CIS	51.7	51.9	52.4	52.8	53.7	54.1	53.4	53.3	53.6	53.8
East Asia	73.5	72.5	71.9	71.4	71.0	70.4	70.0	69.8	69.9	70.1
Latin America and the Caribbean	58.1	59.2	59.9	60.6	60.9	61.3	60.6	60.4	60.7	61.0
Middle East	44.8	44.9	45.1	45.3	45.3	45.1	45.2	45.1	45.4	45.8
North Africa	43.9	45.2	45.4	46.0	46.1	46.5	46.4	46.2	46.6	46.9
South Asia	57.5	58.4	58.5	58.7	58.8	59.0	59.0	58.9	59.1	59.2
Southeast Asia and the Pacific	67.1	65.8	65.6	65.6	66.0	66.0	65.9	65.6	65.8	66.1
Sub-Saharan Africa	63.5	64.2	64.3	64.8	65.1	65.2	65.2	64.9	65.2	65.5

Source: ILO 2011, 63.
Note: Estimates for 2010 are preliminary; CI = confidence interval.

Table 1.3　Vulnerable Employment by Region, 1998–2009

(percent)

Both sexes	1998	1999	2000	2005	2006	2007	2008	2009
World	53.7	53.5	53.3	51.9	51.4	51.0	50.2	50.1
Developed economies and European Union	11.3	11.1	10.8	10.3	10.0	9.9	9.7	9.7
Central and southeastern Europe (non-EU) and CIS	24.1	26.7	25.6	22.8	21.9	20.7	20.4	20.0
East Asia	61.4	60.2	59.1	55.8	55.2	54.5	52.2	50.8
Latin America and the Caribbean	35.7	36.1	35.8	33.8	32.7	32.3	31.8	32.2
Middle East	36.8	36.0	35.7	33.9	33.7	33.3	32.9	32.7
North Africa	43.7	42.1	42.4	42.6	41.1	41.2	40.2	40.4
South Asia	81.9	81.1	82.1	80.5	80.2	79.9	78.9	78.5
Southeast Asia and the Pacific	63.8	66.2	65.5	62.6	62.3	62.0	62.5	61.8
Sub-Saharan Africa	80.5	79.9	79.5	77.1	76.6	76.0	75.3	75.8

Source: ILO 2011, 69.

employment has been roughly flat, with increases in Latin America and the Caribbean, North Africa, and Sub-Saharan Africa.

Roughly 39 percent of workers are considered to be working poor, based on a poverty line of US$2.00 per day, representing 1.2 billion workers worldwide. While significant improvements have been made in reducing poverty—and all developing regions, except Sub-Saharan Africa, western Asia, and parts of Eastern Europe and Central Asia expected to achieve the Millennium Development Goal target of halving the share of people living in extreme poverty (less than US$1.25 per day) by 2015 (ILO 2011, 23)—progress slowed during the crisis, and this is reflected in the numbers of working poor.

Based on a rate of US$1.25 per day, the estimated poverty rate for workers in the global economy in 2009 was 20.7 percent, or one in five. This percentage is higher than the precrisis projected rate of 19.1 percent, representing 40 million more working poor (ILO 2011, 26) (see figure 1.1).

Table 1.4 shows the numbers of working poor and their share in total employment. The numbers of working poor in North Africa have

Figure 1.1   Global Working Poverty Trends, 1999–2009
(based on US$1.25 per day)

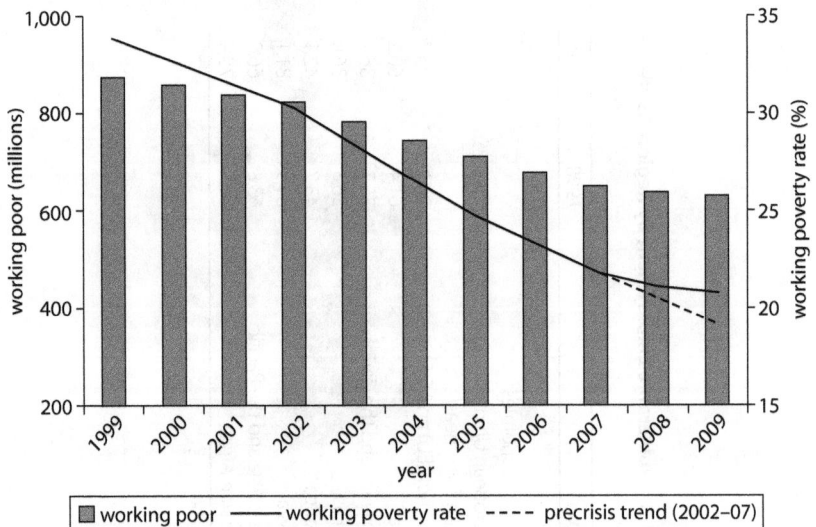

Source: ILO 2011, 24.
Note: Estimates for 2008 and 2009 are preliminary.

Table 1.4 Number and Share of Working Poor by Region, Selected Years, 1999–2009
(based on US$1.25 per day)

Both sexes	Numbers of people (millions)				Share in total employment (%)			
	1999	2003	2008	2009	1999	2003	2008	2009
World	875.1	785.6	640.0	631.9	33.9	28.4	21.1	20.7
Central and southeastern Europe (non-EU) and CIS	10.6	9.3	7.0	7.0	7.3	6.2	4.3	4.3
East Asia	286.2	203.8	83.1	73.0	38.7	26.0	10.3	9.0
Latin America and the Caribbean	26.3	28.0	16.6	17.4	13.0	12.8	6.6	6.9
Middle East	2.8	3.8	3.7	3.7	6.2	7.4	6.0	5.9
North Africa	10.5	11.1	10.5	10.7	21.4	20.2	16.2	16.1
South Asia	285.2	291.7	284.5	282.0	56.6	52.2	44.9	43.5
Southeast Asia and the Pacific	106.0	81.6	64.3	63.6	45.2	32.5	23.3	22.6
Sub-Saharan Africa	147.5	156.2	170.2	174.6	66.9	63.0	58.5	58.5

Source: ILO 2011, 719.
Note: Estimates for 2008 and 2009 are preliminary; percentages may not add to 100 due to rounding.

increased over the 10-year period to 2009, a trend that is particularly visible in the Middle East and Sub-Saharan Africa. The numbers of working poor both at the US$1.25 and at the US$2.00 per day poverty line are vulnerable to further shocks. The ILO (2011, 26) notes that although there is always the possibility that economic recovery will falter, the more likely threat to the working poor and the poor in general is that rising inflation will lead to higher food and commodity prices. Developed-economy governments and central banks must recognize that loose monetary policy may generate inflationary pressures in developing economies through increased capital inflows in search of higher returns. Developing-economy governments and central banks need to be aware of how their own monetary stance and currency regimes may lead to inflationary pressures. Current levels and growth rates of unemployment and employment pose real challenges for the labor market going forward.

Labor Market Trends

This section examines labor market trends in employment, unemployment, labor force participation, wages, and productivity. Both developed and developing countries face difficult challenges.

Employment

Global employment continued to grow during the crisis, albeit at a reduced pace due to the decline in employment experienced by the developed economies and the European Union (EU) (–2.2 percent) and by Central and Eastern Europe (non-EU) and the Commonwealth of Independent States (CIS) (–0.9 percent) (see table 1.5). For many developing countries, employment is driven by demographic trends, as most workers work in the informal economy and the lack of adequate social insurance means that macroeconomic shocks have limited employment impact. Preliminary estimates for 2010 suggest that employment growth will continue to be negative for the developed economies and EU (–0.9 percent) and that the developing regions will experience growth rates close to their 2007 rates.

Unemployment

As noted, global unemployment has been slow to recover in the aftermath of the crisis. The increases in unemployment in 2009 (22 million) were not redressed sufficiently in 2010, and the global unemployment

Table 1.5 Annual Employment Growth by Region, 2001–09
(percent)

Region	2001–06	2007	2008	2009	2010		
					CI lower bound	*Preliminary estimate*	*CI upper bound*
World	1.9	1.8	1.5	0.7	1.0	1.3	1.7
Developed economies and European Union	0.9	1.4	0.6	−2.2	−1.2	−0.9	−0.5
Central and southeastern Europe (non-EU) and CIS	1.0	2.1	1.1	−0.9	0.1	0.6	1.2
East Asia	1.1	0.7	0.2	0.5	0.7	0.9	1.1
Latin America and the Caribbean	2.8	2.2	2.3	0.5	1.5	2.0	2.5
Middle East	3.6	2.9	2.3	3.0	2.1	2.9	3.6
North Africa	3.5	2.6	3.1	2.1	1.7	2.5	3.2
South Asia	2.7	2.4	2.6	2.2	2.0	2.3	2.7
Southeast Asia and the Pacific	1.8	2.5	1.9	1.7	1.3	1.7	2.0
Sub-Saharan Africa	3.2	3.1	3.0	2.6	2.4	2.8	3.2

Source: ILO 2011, 71.
Note: Estimates for 2010 are preliminary; CI = confidence interval.

rate stood at 6.2 percent, marginally better than the 6.3 percent recorded in 2009 (ILO 2011, 12). Table 1.6 shows the unemployment rates by region since 2000 and preliminary estimates for 2010.

Countries in the developed regions continue to experience increasing unemployment. The unemployment rate is estimated to increase by 0.8 percentage point in 2010 for the developed economies and EU (see table 1.6). This increase is in contrast to all other regions (except Sub-Saharan Africa), where the rate of unemployment decreased between 2009 and 2010 (table 1.6). The largest decrease—0.8 percentage point—took place in Central and southeastern Europe (non-EU) and CIS.

Disaggregating the data further shows the unemployment rate by sex and by age. Globally, there is no discernible difference between the sexes with regard to unemployment (the rate of unemployment among men is estimated at 6.0 percent for 2010 and at 6.5 percent for women). Men experienced a higher increase in unemployment during the crisis—an increase of 0.8 percentage point (from 5.4 percent in 2007 to 6.2 percent in 2009) compared to a 0.5-percentage-point increase for women (from 6.0 percent in 2007 to 6.5 percent in 2009) (ILO 2011, 13). This difference was largely attributable to the extensive layoffs in male-dominated industries (construction and financial sectors) in the developed economies and European Union region (ILO 2011, 13).

Table 1.7 shows the rate of youth unemployment by region. Globally, the rate of youth unemployment is estimated to have recovered slightly in 2010 (12.6 percent) from 12.8 percent in 2009 (see table 1.7). The rate is an improvement over the initial estimate of the ILO (ILO 2010), but the decline in the labor force participation by youth suggests a more cautious interpretation. The ILO (2011) suggests that these trends may be due to discouraged workers leaving the labor force, who are not counted as unemployed. The rate of youth unemployment is estimated to have increased in 2010 from the 2009 rate for the developed economies and EU, Southeast Asia and the Pacific, and the Middle East and by a smaller margin in North Africa and Sub-Saharan Africa (table 1.7).

Labor Force Participation Rates
Offsetting effects, such as migration within and between countries, often have little impact on the aggregate regional or global labor force (ILO 2010). Despite the global financial crisis, the labor force participation rate stood at 65.3 percent in 2009, unchanged from the rate in 2007 (see table 1.8). Across the regions, participation rates varied substantially between Central and southeastern Europe (non-EU) and CIS, where it rose by

Table 1.6 Annual Unemployment by Region, 2000–10
(percent)

Both sexes	2000	2004	2005	2006	2007	2008	2009	2010 CI lower bound	2010 Preliminary estimate	2010 CI upper bound
World	6.3	6.4	6.2	5.9	5.6	5.7	6.3	5.9	6.2	6.5
Developed economies and European Union	6.7	7.2	6.9	6.3	5.8	6.1	8.4	8.5	8.8	9.1
Central and southeastern Europe (non-EU) and CIS	10.9	9.9	9.4	9.3	8.6	8.6	10.4	9.1	9.6	10.1
East Asia	4.5	4.3	4.1	4.0	3.8	4.3	4.4	3.9	4.1	4.3
Latin America and the Caribbean	8.5	8.4	7.9	7.6	7.0	6.6	7.7	7.2	7.7	8.1
Middle East	10.6	11.2	11.2	10.7	10.5	10.2	10.3	9.6	10.3	10.9
North Africa	14.1	11.9	11.6	10.5	10.2	9.6	9.9	9.1	9.8	10.5
South Asia	4.5	4.7	4.8	4.6	4.5	4.3	4.4	3.9	4.3	4.6
Southeast Asia and the Pacific	4.9	6.4	6.3	6.0	5.4	5.3	5.2	4.8	5.1	5.4
Sub-Saharan Africa	9.0	8.6	8.6	8.0	7.9	7.9	7.9	7.6	8.0	8.4

Source: ILO, 2011, 61.
Note: Estimates for 2010 are preliminary; CI = confidence interval.

Table 1.7 Youth Unemployment by Region, 2000–10
(percent)

Youth	2000	2004	2005	2006	2007	2008	2009	2010 CI lower bound	2010 Preliminary estimate	2010 CI upper bound
World	12.8	13.0	12.9	12.4	11.8	11.9	12.8	11.9	12.6	13.3
Developed economies and European Union	13.5	14.6	14.2	13.3	12.4	13.3	17.4	17.6	18.2	18.7
Central and southeastern Europe (non-EU) and CIS	20.4	19.9	19.2	19.0	18.1	17.6	20.8	18.1	18.9	20.0
East Asia	9.0	8.6	8.3	8.0	7.7	8.7	8.9	7.9	8.3	8.7
Latin America and the Caribbean	15.7	16.5	15.7	15.3	14.2	13.8	15.7	14.3	15.2	16.1
Middle East	23.7	24.9	25.3	24.4	24.5	24.5	24.9	23.5	25.1	26.7
North Africa	29.5	26.0	26.7	24.4	24.3	22.6	23.4	22.1	23.6	25.1
South Asia	10.2	9.8	10.1	10.0	9.9	9.5	9.9	8.8	9.5	10.2
Southeast Asia and the Pacific	12.9	16.6	17.4	16.8	14.5	14.2	13.9	13.3	14.2	15.0
Sub-Saharan Africa	13.8	13.2	13.1	12.2	12.1	12.1	12.1	11.7	12.3	12.9

Source: ILO 2011, 62.
Note: Estimates for 2010 are preliminary; CI = confidence interval.

0.8 percentage point, and East Asia, where it declined by 0.6 percentage point (table 1.8). These changes are in line with ongoing trends in participation. The rate of labor force participation in East Asia, despite the downward trend since 2000, is the highest of all regions. The rate in the Middle East is the lowest of all the regions, due to the low participation of females in the labor force. Just one in five women in the Middle East works (ILO 2011, 33).

Disaggregating the data by sex and age shows greater disparity among the regions and a greater impact from the global financial crisis. Figure 1.2 from the ILO (2011,15) contrasts the actual outcome in male and female labor force participation rates from 2007 to 2009 with what would have been expected in the absence of the financial crisis for the developed economies and the EU, Central and southeastern Europe (non-EU) and CIS, Southeast Asia and the Pacific, and Latin America and the Caribbean.

Male participation rates declined by more than would have been expected in the absence of the crisis in the developed economies and EU and in Latin America and the Caribbean, while the increase in female labor force participation in these regions was lower than what would have been expected. These estimates suggest increasing numbers of discouraged workers who do not even try to look for employment. Discouraged workers are not counted as part of the unemployed, underscoring the need to examine a range of labor market indicators for a full appreciation of the situation. There was little difference between the actual labor force participation rates by sex and the estimate based on no crisis in Southeast Asia and the Pacific. This finding may reflect the lack of a social safety net, whereby workers seek any type of employment, even in the informal economy. At the other extreme, participation rates in Central and Eastern Europe (non-EU) and the CIS region were higher than would have been expected in the absence of a crisis, suggesting that more workers were pulled into the labor force in the face of the crisis.

A significant gender gap in rates of labor force participation is evident in South Asia, the Middle East, and North Africa. The difference in male and female rates amounts to almost 50 percentage points (see table 1.9). While female participation has increased somewhat over 2000 to 2009, the increase is from a very low base. The greatest increase in female participation took place in Latin America and the Caribbean, rising from 47.3 percent in 2000 to 52.0 percent in 2009. The largest decline in female participation took place in East Asia. Gender differences in

Table 1.8 Labor Force Participation by Region, 2000–09
(percent)

Both sexes	2000	2001	2002	2003	2004	2005	2006	2007	2008	2009
World	65.6	65.5	65.7	65.6	65.5	65.5	65.4	65.3	65.4	65.3
Developed economies and European Union	60.8	60.5	60.3	60.2	60.2	60.3	60.5	60.6	60.8	60.5
Central and southeastern Europe (non-EU) and CIS	56.0	58.1	58.1	57.5	57.6	57.9	58.3	58.8	59.2	59.6
East Asia	77.0	76.7	77.1	76.5	75.8	75.0	74.3	73.8	73.5	73.2
Latin America and the Caribbean	63.6	63.5	63.9	64.0	64.6	65.0	65.6	65.5	65.6	65.6
Middle East	50.1	50.1	50.2	50.4	50.6	50.8	50.7	50.6	50.2	50.4
North Africa	51.1	51.0	51.0	51.2	51.3	51.3	51.4	51.3	51.4	51.5
South Asia	60.1	60.4	60.7	61.0	61.3	51.4	61.6	61.6	61.6	61.7
Southeast Asia and the Pacific	70.6	70.7	70.4	70.4	70.3	70.1	69.8	69.7	69.7	69.5
Sub-Saharan Africa	69.7	69.8	69.9	70.1	70.2	70.4	70.5	70.6	70.8	70.8

Source: ILO 2011, 719.

Sub-Saharan Africa are less than in other regions. The difference in participation rates between men and women was 19.1 percentage points in 2009 and was lower only in East Asia (3.2 percentage points) (table 1.9).

Table 1.10 shows the rate of labor force participation for youth in 2000–09. Globally, the rate has fallen, reflecting greater participation in education or less benignly discouraged workers. All regions except Central and Eastern Europe (non-EU) and CIS experienced a decline in youth participation rates during the crisis, 2007 to 2009. The largest decline—1.3 percentage points—took place in the developed economies and the EU. The smallest decline took place in Sub-Saharan Africa, 0.2 percentage point. North Africa and South Asia also experienced small declines (0.3- and 0.4-percentage-point differences, respectively). These small declines

Figure 1.2   Change in Labor Force Participation in Selected Developing Regions, 2002–07 and 2007–09

(percent)

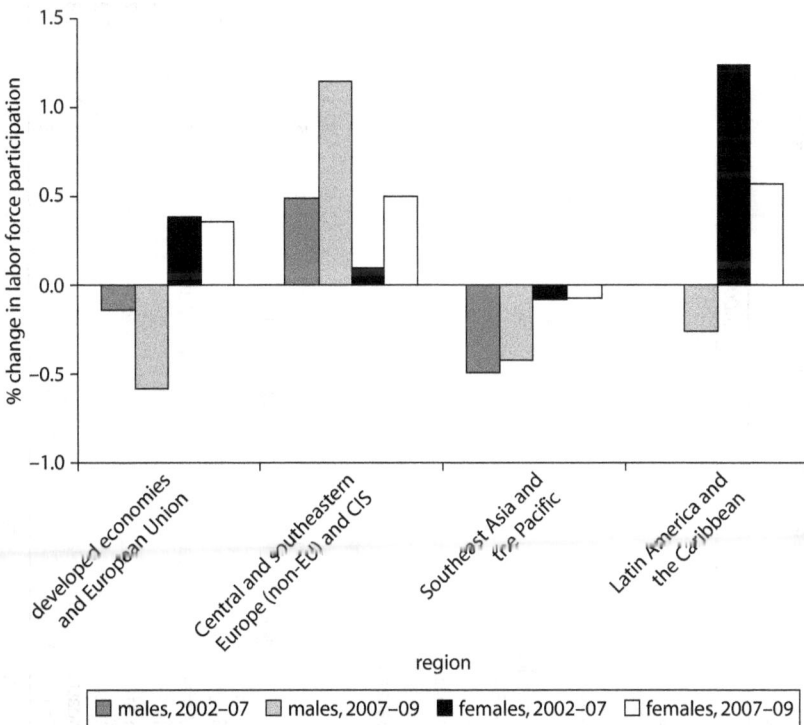

Table 1.9   Male and Female Participation in the Labor Force by Region, 2000–09
(percent)

	2000	2001	2002	2003	2004	2005	2006	2007	2008	2009
Males										
World	79.2	79.0	79.0	78.8	78.7	78.5	78.4	78.2	78.1	77.9
Developed economies and European Union	70.2	69.8	69.4	69.1	68.9	68.9	69.0	69.0	69.0	68.4
Central and southeastern Europe (non-EU) and CIS	68.1	67.9	67.6	67.1	67.5	67.9	68.2	68.6	69.4	69.9
East Asia	83.4	83.1	83.6	83.0	82.3	81.6	80.8	80.2	80.0	79.7
Latin America and the Caribbean	80.6	80.3	80.2	80.0	80.2	80.2	80.5	80.2	80.1	79.9
Middle East	75.1	74.9	74.8	74.8	74.8	75.0	74.6	74.2	73.5	73.7
North Africa	76.2	76.1	75.9	75.8	75.8	75.7	75.7	75.5	75.6	75.6
South Asia	83.3	83.3	83.4	83.4	83.4	83.4	83.3	83.0	82.8	82.6
Southeast Asia and the Pacific	83.5	83.6	83.4	83.3	83.3	82.8	82.5	82.1	81.8	81.7
Sub-Saharan Africa	80.4	80.3	80.3	80.3	80.3	80.3	80.4	80.4	80.6	80.4
Females										
World	52.1	52.1	52.4	52.4	52.4	52.5	52.5	52.6	52.7	52.7
Developed economies and European Union	51.9	51.8	51.7	51.9	52.0	52.2	52.5	52.7	53.0	53.1
Central and southeastern Europe (non-EU) and CIS	49.1	49.4	49.7	49.0	48.8	49.0	49.5	49.9	50.1	50.4
East Asia	70.3	70.0	70.3	69.7	69.0	66.3	67.6	67.2	66.8	66.5
Latin America and the Caribbean	47.3	47.4	48.3	48.7	49.8	50.5	51.4	51.4	51.8	52.0
Middle East	22.6	22.8	23.1	23.4	23.8	24.1	24.3	24.5	24.6	24.8
North Africa	26.2	26.1	26.2	26.7	27.0	27.1	27.2	27.3	27.5	27.6
South Asia	35.5	36.1	36.6	37.2	37.8	36.2	36.6	39.0	39.3	39.6
Southeast Asia and the Pacific	58.1	58.1	57.9	57.8	57.7	57.7	57.5	57.7	57.9	57.6
Sub-Saharan Africa	59.4	59.7	59.9	60.2	60.5	60.7	60.9	61.0	61.3	61.3

Source: ILO 2011, 65.

Table 1.10   Youth Participation in the Labor Force by Region, 2000–09
(percent)

Youth	2000	2001	2002	2003	2004	2005	2006	2007	2008	2009
World	53.6	53.1	52.9	52.5	52.4	52.2	52.0	51.7	51.4	51.1
Developed economies and European Union	52.8	51.8	50.9	50.0	49.9	50.0	50.3	50.0	49.9	48.7
Central and southeastern Europe (non-EU) and CIS	43.0	42.5	41.9	40.5	40.5	40.7	41.0	41.5	43.2	43.7
East Asia	65.9	64.7	64.5	63.6	62.7	61.9	61.1	60.6	59.9	59.5
Latin America and the Caribbean	54.5	53.8	53.8	53.3	53.9	53.6	53.8	53.2	53.0	52.7
Middle East	36.1	36.1	36.1	36.2	36.3	36.4	35.8	35.3	34.6	34.5
North Africa	39.0	38.8	38.6	38.9	39.0	38.9	37.9	36.9	36.8	36.6
South Asia	48.4	48.6	48.8	48.9	48.9	48.9	48.9	48.5	48.3	48.1
Southeast Asia and the Pacific	57.5	57.2	56.6	56.1	55.8	55.2	54.2	53.4	52.8	52.3
Sub-Saharan Africa	55.6	55.6	55.6	55.5	55.6	55.6	55.6	55.7	55.7	55.5

Source: ILO 2011, 66.

suggest that individuals cannot afford not to work in regions with little or no social protection.

Productivity and Wages

Labor productivity and real wages provide valuable information on the quality of employment in an economy. Increased productivity may lead to higher wages or reduced working hours for the same pay. Growth in productivity is necessary for poverty reduction (ILO 2011). Labor is the main asset of the poor, but low productivity and low wages make it difficult to move out of poverty, as the large numbers of working poor attest. Increases in the average real wage, however, suggest that the purchasing power of the average worker is increasing.

Productivity is measured here as output per worker, and, together with growth in employment, it sheds light on the quality and quantity of employment being generated. Examining these two indicators for 2007 and 2009 (see figure 1.3) shows the impact of the crisis on regions and globally—"whether employment growth was more severely impacted by the crisis than productivity growth, or vice versa" (ILO 2011, 18). Globally, employment growth continued in 2009 but was not matched by growth in labor productivity. The latter indicator turned negative and declined by 1.4 percent (ILO 2011, 18). Employment growth was starkly negative for the developed economies and EU in 2009, and labor productivity growth turned negative as well. In the Central and southeastern European (non-EU) and CIS countries, the negative employment growth in 2009 was accompanied by a sharp drop in labor productivity growth (see figure 1.3). East Asia, South Asia, and North Africa all experienced slower employment growth and slower labor productivity growth in 2009 compared with 2007, but the indicators remained positive. Elsewhere—Southeast Asia and the Pacific, Latin America and the Caribbean, and Sub-Saharan Africa—employment growth declined and became negative in 2009 compared to 2007; but labor productivity remained positive in 2009, albeit at a slower growth rate than before (2007) (figure 1.3).

Average wages continued to grow during the crisis but at a decelerating rate. Globally, average real monthly wages grew by 0.7 percent in 2009, compared to 0.8 percent in 2008 and 2.2 percent in 2007. Among the developed economies and the EU, average monthly wages accelerated by 0.6 percent in 2009 compared to a decline of 0.5 percent in 2008 and growth of 0.8 percent in 2007 (ILO 2011, 14). Further data from the ILO show that real wages in Central and Eastern Europe (non-EU) and

Figure 1.3   World and Regional Growth in Labor Productivity and Employment, 2007 and 2009
(percent)

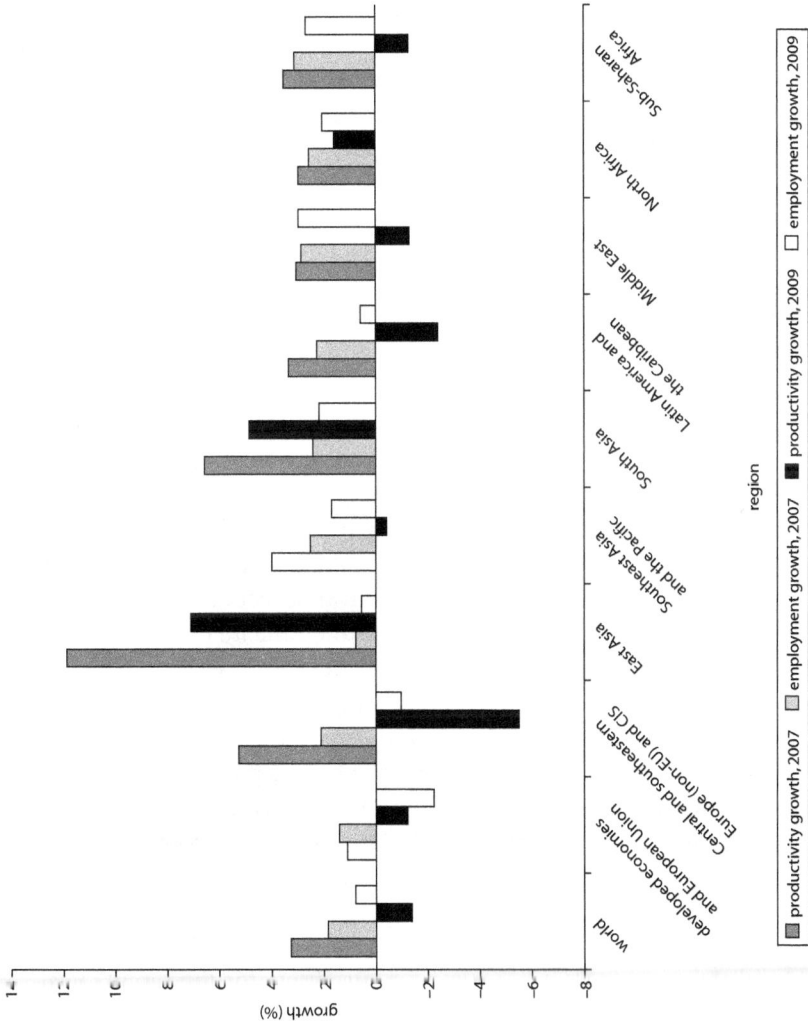

Source: ILO 2011, 18.

CIS grew 6.6 percent in 2007 and 4.6 percent in 2008 and then declined 0.1 percent in 2009 (ILO 2011, 14). The ILO notes that there was evidence of large wage inequality even before the crisis.

The joint report of the ILO and the International Monetary Fund (IMF) on employment noted the widening inequality in the distribution of wages worldwide. For some countries, such as the United Kingdom and the United States, the inequality comes from the concentrated distribution of income in the top deciles, while for many developing and transition countries, widening wage inequality stems from falling earnings among low-wage earners (ILO-IMF 2010, 62). Some countries, in the face of a widening distribution of wages and the aftermath of the financial crisis, are examining again their minimum wage legislation (ILO-IMF 2010, 76).[2] Furthermore, in labor market policy, collective bargaining arrangements are associated with reduced wage inequality (ILO-IMF 2010, 78).

Employment by sector. Globally, the share of agricultural employment has been declining (see table 1.11),[3] falling by 5.2 percentage points between 1999 and 2009, while that of services has been increasing, rising from 39.1 percent in 1999 to 43.2 percent in 2009. The share of industrial employment increased by 1.5 percentage points between 1999 and 2008 and declined by 0.3 percentage point in 2009, reflecting the heavy impact of the financial crisis on the industrial sector.

Agricultural employment continues to dominate overall employment in East Asia, Southeast Asia and the Pacific, South Asia, and Sub-Saharan Africa, which has the highest share of agricultural employment of the developing regions. Employment in the service sector is particularly visible in the developed economies and the EU, accounting for 72.8 percent of all employment in 2009; that share has increased by 5.9 percentage points since 1999 (see table 1.9). Among the developing regions, the service sector dominates in Latin America and the Caribbean (61.6 percent of total employment was in services in 2009), the Middle East (54.8 percent), and North Africa (49.7 percent) (see table 1.11). The share of industrial employment has also been increasing for the sample years for all the developing regions and accounts for over one-fifth of total employment in East Asia, Latin America and the Caribbean, the Middle East, and North Africa (see table 1.11).

Globally, industrial employment was the hardest hit during the crisis. Before 2007, industrial employment grew by 3.4 percent per year over the period 2002–07 (ILO 2011, 21) (see figure 1.4). In 2009, global

Table 1.11 Sectoral Employment Share by Region, Selected Years, 1999–2009
(percent)

Both sexes	Agriculture				Industry				Services			
	1999	*2007*	*2008*	*2009*	*1999*	*2007*	*2008*	*2009*	*1999*	*2007*	*2008*	*2009*
World	40.2	35.4	35.0	35.0	20.6	22.1	22.1	21.8	39.1	42.5	42.9	43.2
Developed economies and European Union	5.6	3.9	3.7	3.7	27.6	25.0	24.6	23.4	66.9	71.1	71.7	72.8
Central and southeastern Europe (non-EU) and CIS	27.0	20.0	20.2	20.2	24.5	25.6	25.2	24.6	48.5	54.5	54.6	55.2
East Asia	47.9	38.9	37.7	36.9	23.8	27.1	27.5	27.8	28.3	33.9	34.8	35.3
Latin America and the Caribbean	21.5	17.0	16.4	16.3	21.4	22.6	22.8	22.1	57.1	60.5	60.8	61.6
Middle East	22.1	20.5	19.5	19.1	25.9	26.5	26.1	26.1	52.1	53.1	54.4	54.8
North Africa	29.2	28.4	28.0	27.8	20.5	21.8	22.2	22.5	50.3	49.8	49.7	49.7
South Asia	59.5	53.5	53.5	53.5	15.4	18.9	18.9	18.9	25.1	27.6	27.6	27.6
Southeast Asia and the Pacific	49.3	45.0	44.7	44.3	15.9	18.0	17.8	17.8	34.8	37.0	37.5	38.0
Sub-Saharan Africa	62.4	59.4	58.9	59.0	8.8	10.4	10.6	10.6	28.8	30.2	30.5	30.4

Source: ILO 2011, 67.

Figure 1.4   Average Annual Percentage Change in Regional Employment by Sector, 2002–07 and 2008–09

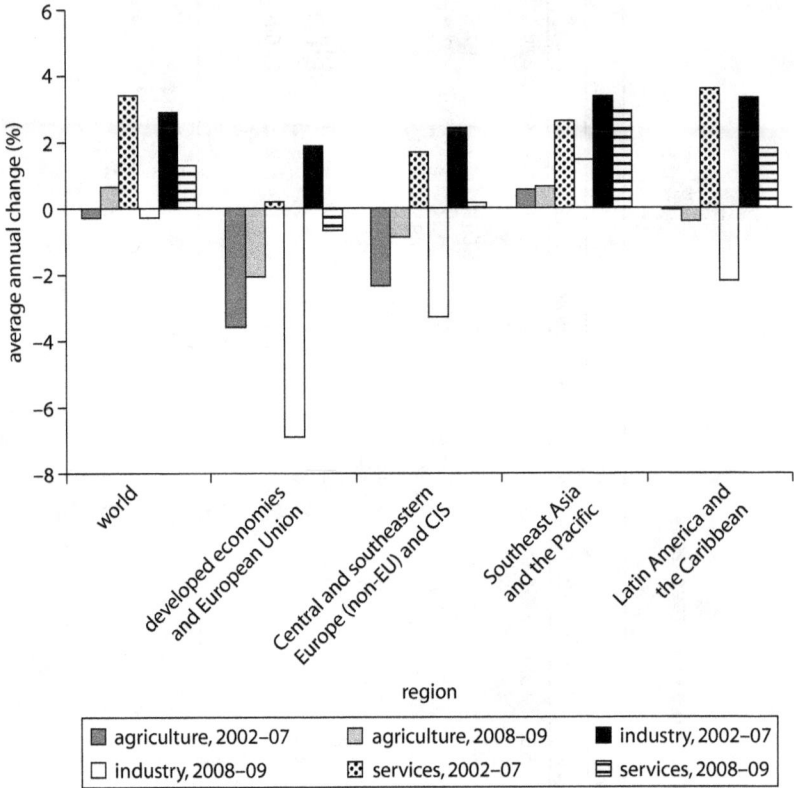

region

Legend		
■ agriculture, 2002–07	▨ agriculture, 2008–09	■ industry, 2002–07
□ industry, 2008–09	⊠ services, 2002–07	⊟ services, 2008–09

Source: ILO 2011, 21.

industrial employment declined. Developed economies and the European Union were the worst-hit regions, with employment in industry declining by almost 7 percent (see figure 1.4). Industrial employment also declined substantially in Central and southeastern Europe (non-EU) and CIS and in Latin America and the Caribbean (figure 1.4).

Gender and the Labor Market

The gender gap is at its most obvious in the labor market, where women often face greater barriers than men in securing decent and productive work. Often men and women are segregated into gender roles because of tradition or specialization. In other regions, cultural reasons dictate the occupations that women may take up, if any. Child bearing is the preserve of women, which may keep them out of the labor market. While the segregation of women's roles is changing (ILO 2007), women are more likely to be employed in agriculture (in developing economies) and service sector work (see table 1.12). The data for service sector employment in table 1.12 indicate that the gender gap between males and females is increasing over time, while staying more or less the same for agricultural employment. Across the developing regions, the gap is even more evident, with 76.9 percent of women employed in the service sector in Latin America and the Caribbean compared to 51.5 percent of men (ILO 2011, 69).

Women's participation in the labor market has increased (table 1.12), standing at 52.9 percent in 2009. This increase has occurred in most regions, although not in East Asia or in Southeast Asia and the Pacific, which show a decrease in female participation.[4] The gender gap in labor force participation is substantial for the Middle East and North Africa.[5] Moreover, as Nallari and Griffith observe, "The quality of work and working conditions has not always kept pace with increases in participation. Persistent gender inequalities in wages suggest that the labor market is not operating freely" (2011, 101).

Women make up at least 60 percent of the world's working poor (ILO 2004), and women are overrepresented in informal work. The global vulnerable employment rate for women stood at 51.8 percent in 2009, compared to a rate of 48.9 percent for males. The global rates hide disparity among the developing regions. For example, there is a 21.8-percentage point-difference between the female and the male rate of vulnerable employment in North Africa (ILO 2011, 69).[6]

Table 1.12   Global Labor Market Indicators by Sex, 2000, 2007, and 2009
(percent)

Indicator	2000		2007		2009	
	Male	Female	Male	Female	Male	Female
Employment to population rate	74.3	48.6	74.0	49.4	73.1	49.2
Unemployment rate	6.1	6.6	5.4	6.0	6.2	6.5
Labor force participation rate	79.2	52.1	78.2	52.6	77.9	52.9
Vulnerable employment rate	51.8	55.5	49.5	53.2	48.9	51.8
Agricultural employment (share)	38.3[a]	43.2[a]	33.6	38.2	33.3	37.6
Industrial employment (share)	24.3[a]	15.1[a]	26.3	15.9	26.0	15.6
Service employment (share)	37.5[a]	41.9[a]	40.1	46.0	40.7	46.8

Source: ILO 2011, 59–71.
a. Data are for 1999.

Conclusion

The chapter examined key trends in the global labor market, having first discussed the impact of the recent global financial crisis on employment. The labor market has yet to recover from the financial crisis, especially in the developed economies and the European Union, where unemployment remains stubbornly high. This high unemployment poses severe costs, including reduced lifetime earnings, diminished employability, and negative health and social effects.[7] The following trends were noted:

- The employment-to-population ratio, a measure of the quantity of employment being generated, continues to fall.
- The decline in vulnerable employment was interrupted by the financial crisis, but vulnerable employment is now expected to increase further. Vulnerable employment is particularly stark in South Asia and Sub-Saharan Africa, reflecting the high incidence of agricultural employment in these regions.
- The numbers of working poor have increased in the wake of the crisis.
- Employment continued to grow during the crisis but at a slower rate. Employment growth will continue to be negative for the developed economies and the EU. Employment growth for the developing economies depends primarily on demographics, as social protection is limited or nonexistent—workers have no choice.
- Unemployment remains above precrisis levels. There are no differences in unemployment between the sexes, but youth unemployment has been increasing. Also of concern is the declining labor force participation among youth, suggesting that many are becoming discouraged and leaving the labor market.
- Globally, labor force participation remains stable. At a disaggregated level, a substantial gender gap is evident in the Middle East and North Africa regions.
- Labor productivity and average real wages—two indicators of the quality of employment being generated—have declined in the wake of the crisis. Moreover, wage inequality has been increasing, even in the years before the crisis.

A final section commented on the gender gap in the labor market. This discrepancy is most evident with regard to vulnerable employment, labor force participation rates, and sectoral employment across the developing regions in particular. Developments in agriculture pose challenges for the labor market, given the large share of the working poor and women in particular who are employed in subsistence agriculture.

Notes

1. "Real global GDP, private consumption, gross fixed investment and world trade had all recovered by 2010, surpassing pre-crisis levels" (ILO 2011, ix).
2. The minimum wage is around 40 percent of the average industrial wage in most countries. Before the crisis, minimum wages were increasing in developed countries. Post-2007, some countries have decided to hold the level, while others, for example, Brazil, decided to increase the rate (with no impact on employment) (ILO-IMF 2010, 76).
3. "The number of workers in agriculture actually grew over the past decade, though the share of workers in the sector declined as employment grew at a faster rate in the other sectors" (ILO 2011, 20).
4. The female labor force participation ratio was 70.3 in 2000 in East Asia, falling to 66.3 in 2009. The rates for Southeast Asia and the Pacific were 58.1 percent (2000) and 57.6 percent (2009) (ILO 2011, 66).
5. Female labor force participation rates in the Middle East and North Africa in 2009 were 24.8 and 27.6 percent, respectively, compared to male labor force participation rates of 73.7 percent (Middle East) and 75.6 percent (North Africa) (ILO 2011, 65–66).
6. Female vulnerable employment in North Africa in 2009 was 56.7 percent, while the male rate was 34.9 percent (ILO 2011, 69).
7. ILO 2011, xii.

References

ILO (International Labour Organization). 2004. *Global Employment Trends for Women 2004*. Geneva: ILO.

———. 2007. *Global Employment Trends for Women Brief*. Geneva: ILO.

———. 2010. *Global Employment Trends*. Geneva: ILO.

———. 2011. *Global Employment Trends*. Geneva: ILO.

ILO-IMF (International Monetary Fund). 2010. "The Challenges of Growth, Employment and Social Cohesion." Joint ILO-IMF conference in cooperation with the Office of the Prime Minister of Norway. Discussion Document, http://www.osloconference2010.org/discussionpaper.pdf.

Nallari, R., and B. Griffith. 2011. *Gender and Macroeconomic Policy: Directions in Development*. Washington, DC: World Bank.

CHAPTER 2

Job Creation

The adverse impact on employment of the global financial crisis that began in late 2007 and continued to early 2009 persists. Among the developed economies, unemployment remains stubbornly high. Although recovery has taken place in the export sector of developing and transition economies, informal employment and the numbers of working poor have increased. Furthermore, there have been large increases in youth unemployment. Evidence from the global labor market suggests a slow, jobless recovery.

The challenge facing the different types of economies—developing, transition, and developed—is to generate sufficient capacity to create jobs and achieve strong, sustainable growth. This outcome will rely on a stable macroeconomic environment and also on the strengthening of labor markets and labor market institutions in the underlying economies.

This chapter will first examine possible channels of job creation. It will then turn to a discussion of strengthening labor market institutions to better facilitate sustainable job creation.

Channels of Job Creation

A number of factors affect job creation in national economies and in individual firms.[1] Chief among these is the prevailing macroeconomic environment. This factor has been identified by the World Bank in its MILES Framework (discussed in chapter 3) as one of the five that affect employment and, together with investment, as one of the two main factors affecting job creation. Labor institutions and aspects of labor policies also affect job creation. The third factor is industrial policy. Labor demand and supply are also affected by globalization.

Macroeconomic Environment

A stable, growing macroeconomic environment is critical for job creation. The global financial crisis dealt a severe shock to the macroeconomy in developing and developed countries with adverse effects for the labor market. A joint publication of the International Labour Organization (ILO) and the International Monetary Fund (IMF) (ILO-IMF 2010) refers to the period as "the great recession of 2007–09," with over 210 million unemployed in 2010, an increase of 30 million since 2007. Unemployment has been pervasive, especially in the advanced economies where the rate of unemployment has increased by three percentage points since 2007, compared to 0.25 percentage point in emerging markets (ILO-IMF 2010). The increase in the unemployment rate varied substantially—climbing by almost 10 percentage points in the case of New Zealand; Spain; Taiwan, China; and the United States—to barely moving in the case of Germany and Norway. Cross-country differences were due to the macroeconomic environment. The increase in the rate of unemployment reflected several factors:

- The extent of the fall in aggregate demand
- The coincidence of the decline in aggregate demand with acute stresses in other sectors, for example, the financial and housing sectors
- The extent to which countries used active labor market policies such as short-term work schemes

Of even greater concern has been the unprecedented increase in youth unemployment. An estimated 81 million youth were unemployed in 2009, a record number. The rate of unemployment for those between the ages of 15 and 24 has historically been two to three times greater than the adult rate. In the wake of the crisis, this rate has increased substantially, undoing the improvements made before 2007 (see figure 2.1).

Youth in advanced regions have been worst hit: youth unemployment in Spain doubled from under 20 percent to almost 40 percent (ILO-IMF 2010). The crisis affected those aged 15 to 24 primarily through rising

Figure 2.1   Global Youth Employment, 2000–11

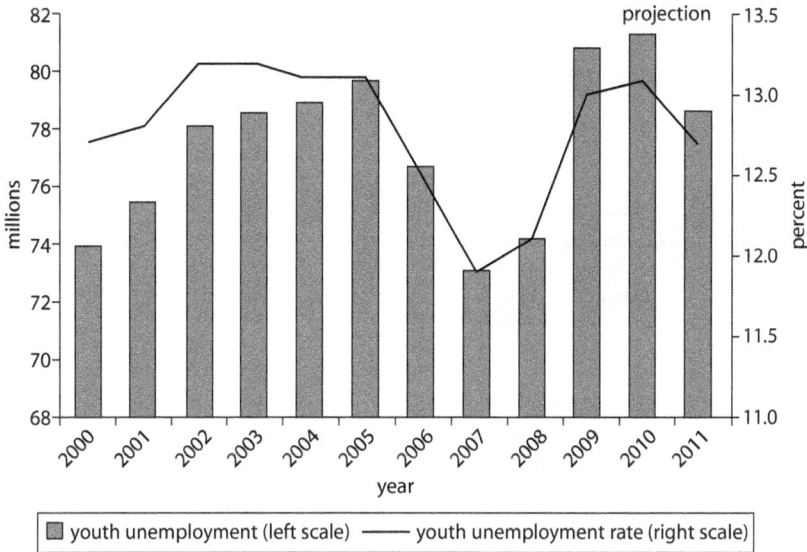

Source: Elder 2010, 26.

unemployment. Figure 2.2 shows youth unemployment in advanced and emerging market economies. Youth unemployment in the advanced and emerging market economies is higher than the global rates. Governments in advanced economies need to ensure that youth unemployment does not turn into entrenched long-term unemployment.

Because in low-income and developing economies youth have little choice but to accept any work they can get, the unemployment numbers appear less grim. Social security safety nets do not provide unemployment benefits to those searching for jobs. Thus, employment-to-population ratios are higher in low-income countries where most of the young men (and women) have to work to support household income (see figure 2.3). Much of this work is in the informal economy where workers fail to make enough money to lift themselves out of poverty. The number of youth classified as working poor[2] was around 152 million in 2008, or 28 percent of global working youth. Most of these workers are poorly educated and work primarily in the agricultural sector (Elder 2010, 27).

The ILO-IMF report suggests a three-part strategy for reducing unemployment worldwide, continuing the approach adopted during the crisis. The applicability and suitability of the relevant parts will depend on the pace of recovery and the country context. Increasing and maintaining

Figure 2.2   Youth Employment in Advanced and Emerging Market Economies, 2007–11
(percent)

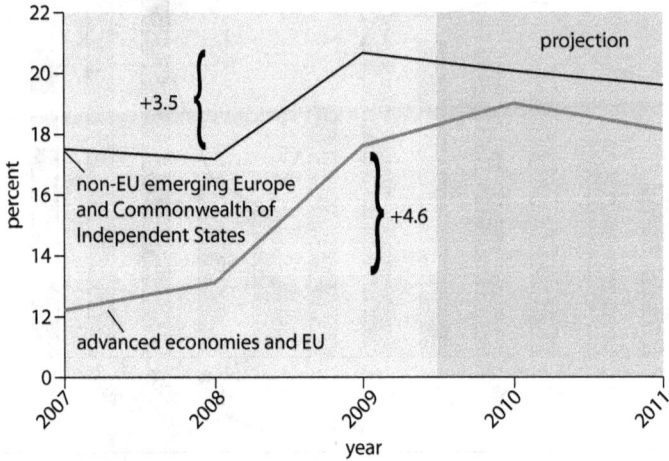

Source: Elder 2010, 26.

aggregate demand are the single-best cure for unemployment (ILO-IMF 2010, 6) and represent the first part of the strategy. Easing the pain is the second part, with jobs recovery as the third:

- *Maintaining support for aggregate demand.* Both fiscal and monetary policies have a role to play in this regard. Fiscal policy should remain expansionary; consolidating spending (before 2011) could hinder recovery. Each country will determine its own adjustments in structural spending, depending on the available fiscal space. Monetary policy should also remain accommodative in supporting aggregate demand. Inflationary pressures continue to be low. Monetary policy should be the first line of defense in advanced economies if growth is challenged.
- *Easing the pain.* Employment subsidies were used to good effect during the crisis, but dependence on these subsidies generates moral hazard. Accordingly, the 2010 ILO-IMF report suggests a phasing out of these policies. Where they still remain critical, the report suggests pairing them with job training to maintain some attachment to the labor force.
- *Jobs recovery.* Despite the moral hazard, job subsidies for hiring can be justified in the aftermath of such a crisis. Most countries have adopted

Figure 2.3   Male Youth-to-Employment Ratios, 1991–2009

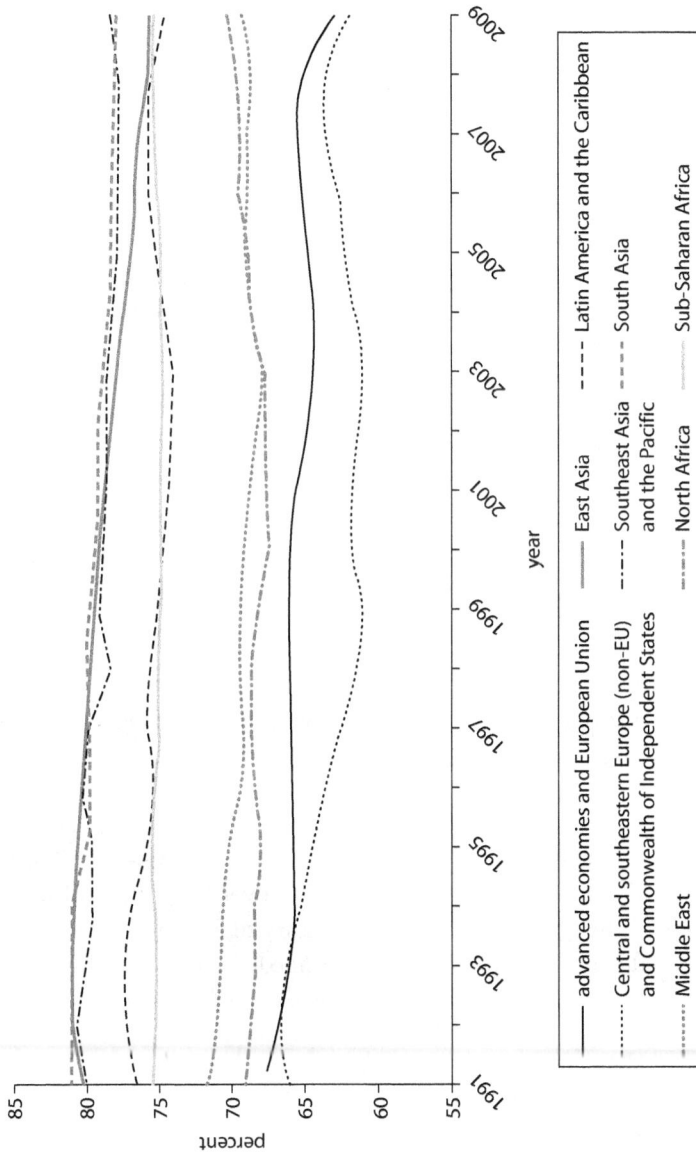

Legend:
- advanced economies and European Union
- Central and southeastern Europe (non-EU) and Commonwealth of Independent States
- Middle East
- East Asia
- Southeast Asia and the Pacific
- North Africa
- Latin America and the Caribbean
- South Asia
- Sub-Saharan Africa

x-axis: year (1991, 1993, 1995, 1997, 1999, 2001, 2003, 2005, 2007, 2009)
y-axis: percent (55, 60, 65, 70, 75, 80, 85)

Source: Elder 2010, 27.

specific subsidy targets to reduce misallocation. The report favors their continued, targeted use for groups most hit by the crisis and those unlikely to be rehired in the absence of these subsidies.

The macroeconomic environment also has a large role to play in building employment. In the 10 years since 1999, global employment grew by roughly 0.47 billion, reaching 3.21 billion in 2009. More than 45 million job seekers are added to the global labor force every year. Pressures from the advanced economies include an aging population and increased dependency ratios. Before the crisis, there was concern with the diminishing share of wages in national income, increasing inequality within wage incomes, and technological change. Income and wage inequality is driven largely by increased income for those at the very top of the income distribution. These inequalities are affected by globalization and a move toward more flexible contracts, workers having less power and less voice. In turn, aggregate demand is affected, and national and international imbalances arise. Most of the employment in the developing regions, in particular, South Asia and Sub-Saharan Africa, is in the informal sector. Those working in the informal sector and the working poor have increased in numbers since the crisis. The need for good employment—"more productive jobs offering better earnings" (ILO-IMF 2008, 7)—is more critical now than ever.

Investment

Investment is one of the main microeconomic instruments affecting job creation. It is part of the MILES Framework identified by the World Bank for the analysis of factors affecting labor demand and supply. In the context of job creation, investment refers to the factors affecting firms' decisions about hiring, firing, and thriving in business. As Smith and Hallward-Driemeier observe, "Firms create over 90 percent of jobs, supply most of the goods and services necessary to improve living standards, and provide the bulk of the tax base needed to fund public services" (2005, 40). This section looks at the external factors affecting firm investment. In 2001, the World Bank launched an annual survey of firms—the Investment Climate Survey[3]—to chart the constraints facing firms, including corruption, finance, regulation, taxation, infrastructure, and labor. Quantitative data collected allow for the construction of an investment climate indicator that, in turn, can be used to assess firm performance in relation to productivity, investment, and employment decisions (Smith and Hallward-Driemeier 2005, 41). In addition, the World Bank maintains the Doing Business Project,[4] which reports on the costs of doing business for a hypothetical firm based on the views of selected experts—accountants, lawyers, and others—in particular countries. The information collected examines the time and cost of doing business.[5] These databases have been used in a number of studies of the investment climate and the results are discussed below.

The *World Development Report* (WDR) (2004) was the first to bring together the results of the two surveys in commenting on the investment climate. Smith and Hallward-Driemeier (2005) present a summary of the report. Firms assessed the investment climate according to a number of factors: risks, costs, and barriers to competition (see figure 2.4).

Policy-related risks are the dominant concern of firms in developing economies. According to Smith and Hallward-Driemeier, "Improving policy predictability alone can increase the likelihood of new investment by more than 30 percent" (2005, 41). Firms are uncertain about the content and implementation of government policies. Firms also identified

Figure 2.4   Factors with an Impact on the Investment Climate

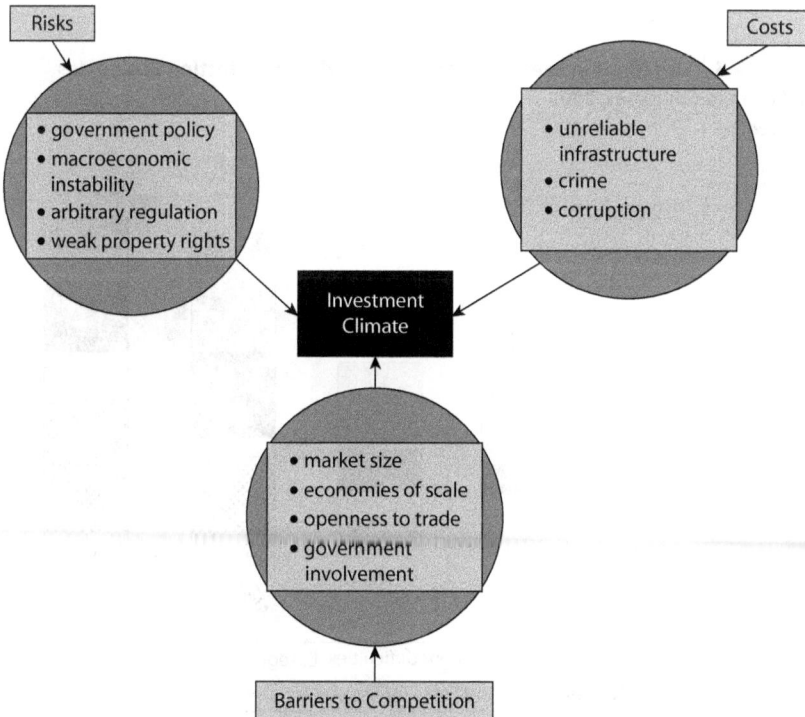

Risks

Costs

- government policy
- macroeconomic instability
- arbitrary regulation
- weak property rights

- unreliable infrastructure
- crime
- corruption

Investment Climate

- market size
- economies of scale
- openness to trade
- government involvement

Barriers to Competition

Source: Compiled from information in Smith and Hallward-Driemeier 2005, 41.

macroeconomic instability, arbitrary regulation, and weak protection of property rights as issues. Among the firms surveyed, almost 90 percent in Guatemala and more than 70 percent in Belarus and Zambia, for example, cited the interpretation of regulations as unpredictable. Firms in Bangladesh (80 percent), Ecuador (70 percent), and Moldova (70 percent) lack confidence that the courts will uphold their property rights (Smith and Hallward-Driemeier 2005, 41). The Investment Climate Survey found that complying with regulation places a large cost on businesses and that the costs associated with infrastructure, crime, and corruption were particularly onerous. Costs arising from unreliable infrastructure are particularly constraining for Algeria and Tanzania (see figure 2.5). As shown in figure 2.5, the combination of weak contract enforcement, arduous regulation, and the costs identified in figure 2.4 can amount to over 25 percent of sale, or "more than three times what firms typically pay in taxes" (Smith and Hallward-Driemeier 2005, 41).[6]

The third adverse factor affecting the investment climate is "barriers to competition." Competition is good for innovation: it promotes productivity and is ultimately good for society. Smith and Hallward-Driemeier

Figure 2.5   Variations in Level and Composition of Costs Affecting Businesses in Selected Countries, 2005

(percent)

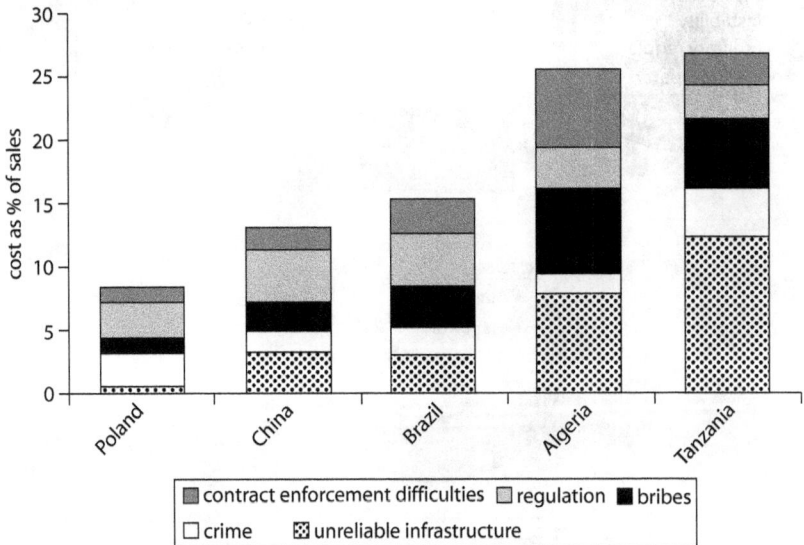

Source: Smith and Hallward-Driemeier 2005, 41.

(2005, 41) citing the WDR noted that stronger competitive pressure can increase the probability of innovation by more than 50 percent. A number of factors affect competition. One such factor is economies of scale and market size. Government can alleviate competitive pressures by regulating market entry and exit and by dealing with anticompetitive behavior. Openness to trade is an avenue through which competition is fostered. Competitive pressure varies among countries: roughly 90 percent of firms in Poland report strong competitive pressure, compared to 45 percent of firms in Georgia (Smith and Hallward-Driemeier 2005, 42).

Rutkowski and Scarpetta (2005) carried out a large-scale study of the factors necessary for enhancing job opportunities in Eastern Europe and the Russian Federation. The chapter on investment climate and job creation came to conclusions similar to those of the WDR (2005), with respect to the factors adversely affecting the investment climate (see figure 2.6).

Rutkowski and Scarpetta (2005) examine the impact of the investment climate on job creation in the region by focusing on two interrelated questions:

Figure 2.6   Major Obstacles to Operations as Reported by Firms in Eastern Europe and the Russian Federation, 2005
(percent)

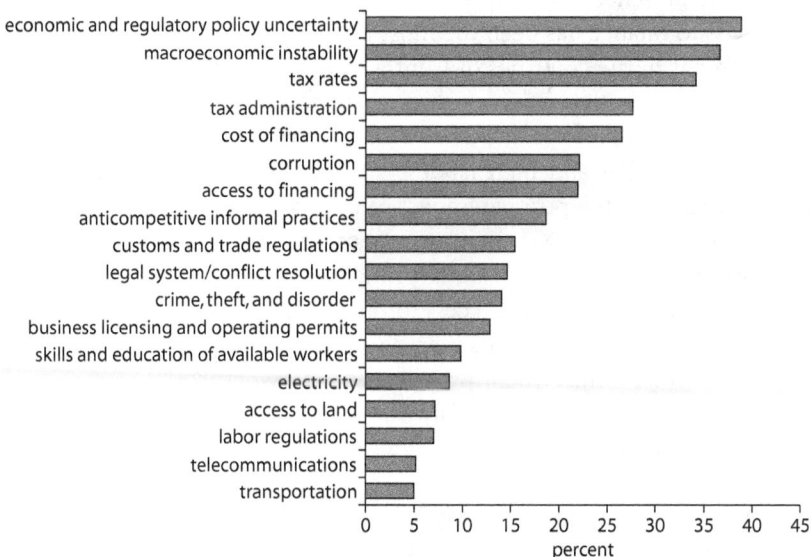

Source: Rutkowski and Scarpetta 2005, 159.

- Do countries with better investment climates have better labor market performance?
- Which institutions are most important for a good employment record?

Using employment in the market services sector as a proxy for private sector employment, the authors examine the effect of various components of the investment climate, adjusted for gross domestic product (GDP) per capita (see table 2.1). Results from the multivariate regression analysis, using service sector employment as a proxy for the private sector, indicate that cross-country differences in employment are due to the prevailing investment climate. The first row of numbers in the table shows actual change in service sector employment, corrected by GDP per capita. All countries except Lithuania[7] show an increase in service sector employment above the one implied by economic development. The second row of numbers shows the predicted change in service sector employment from the model, given the impact of the time shock, country-specific effect, and investment climate in the country. The model performs well for the new countries of the European Union (EU) (see column 2) and less well for the others when comparing actual with predicted change in service sector employment. The authors suggest that this outcome is due to favorable institutions. Results for the other countries reflect the presence of corruption and ineffective legal systems.

Access to finance has been the most important driver of private sector employment in the countries of Central and Eastern Europe and the EU (column 1). The other columns show that access to finance also contributed to the good performance in Hungary, Latvia, and Slovenia, although a high tax burden and high labor market regulations in Hungary and Slovenia reduced the positive impact of private sector employment.

Among the accession countries, labor market regulation and low administrative barriers have been primarily responsible for the rise in private sector employment. Access to finance has, however, hindered the gains in employment. Romania is an illustrative case, whereby the change in private sector employment was smaller than what would be expected given its GDP per capita, primarily due to poor access to finance.[8]

Private sector employment has suffered in Russia and Ukraine because of labor market regulations, start-up costs, and poor access to finance. The positive influence of the relatively low tax burden in these countries was unable to generate sufficient gains in private sector employment in the presence of these constraints on the investment climate. The results

Table 2.1 Multivariate Regression Analysis Showing Contribution of Investment Climate Components to Change in Service Sector Employment in Countries of Central and Eastern Europe and the European Union, 1993–2002

	Average for Central and Eastern Europe, EU member countries	Of which						Average for Central and Eastern Europe, EU accession countries[a]	Of which, Romania (1984–2002)	Average for Russia-Ukraine
		Lithuania (1997–2002)	Hungary (1992–2002)	Slovak Republic (1994–2002)	Poland (1994–2002)	Latvia (1996–2002)	Slovenia (1993–2002)			
Actual change in service sector employment	1.08	−1.83	1.11	0.66	1.33	1.89	0.61	1.06	−0.08	
Predicted change in service sector employment	1.09	0.13	1.92	0.42	1.51	1.26	0.98	0.76	0.30	0.39
Of which:										
Time shock	0.97	0.10	1.42	1.08	1.08	0.44	1.33	0.81	1.08	0.81
Start-up costs	−0.13	0.03	−0.57	−0.16	−0.26	0.17	0.02	0.23	0.53	−0.16
Access to finance	0.44	−0.02	0.70	0.02	0.52	0.39	1.03	−0.50	−1.75	−0.25
Market regulation	0.08	−0.01	1.00	−0.36	0.06	0.14	−0.53	0.15	0.06	−0.35
Tax burden	−0.26	0.04	−0.63	−0.16	0.11	0.12	−0.87	0.06	0.37	0.34

Source: Rutkowski and Scarpetta 2005, 169.

Note: Only statistically significant explanatory variables are shown in the table; corruption and the quality of the legal system were not statistically significant, on average, and are therefore excluded. Low-income CIS countries and Estonia were not included because of lack of data. The averages for country groups are the unweighted average of the estimated contribution of each explanatory variable to the rise in market service employment within the group.

a. Bulgaria, Croatia, and Romania.

presented in table 2.1 suggest that access to finance is the most important determinant of private sector employment in the region,[9] a finding illustrated in figure 2.7.

Access to finance alone is not sufficient to ensure the full potential of private sector employment. Other aspects of the investment climate also remain critical: the tax burden, administrative barriers to firm creation, and labor market regulation. A set of policies that targets these factors together is necessary for employment creation.

Industrial Policy

Direct intervention by the government in the economy to promote industry is experiencing a rebirth. Frowned upon by the Washington Consensus that championed macroeconomic stability, deregulated markets, globalization, and market-based growth during the 1980s and 1990s, there was little, if any, room for industrial policy in the Country Institutional Policy Assessments of the World Bank and the Poverty Reduction Strategy Program of the IMF.[10] A more active role for government is suggested by "new structural economics" and the global financial

Figure 2.7   Effect of Credit Access and Cost on Market Service Employment in Selected Countries in Central and Eastern Europe, 2004

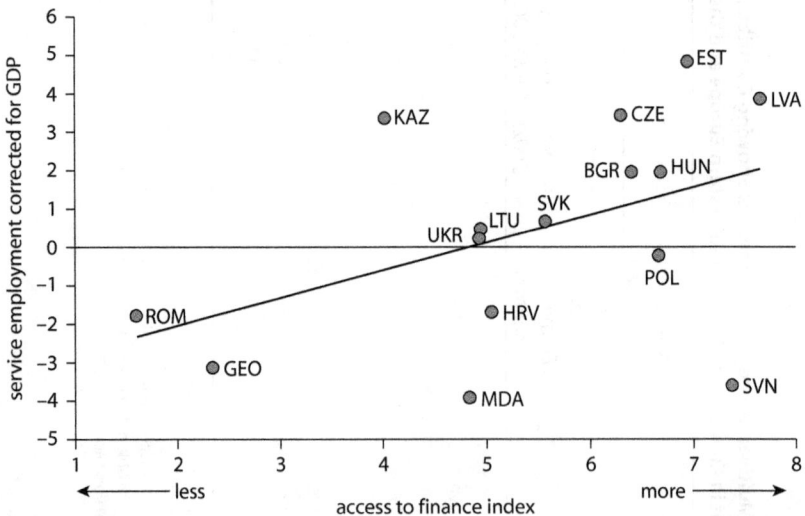

Source: Rutkowski and Scarpetta 2005, 171.
Note: BGR = Bulgaria; CZE = Czech Republic; EST = Estonia; GEO = Georgia; HRV = Bosnia and Herzegovina; HUN = Hungary; KAZ = Kazakhstan; LVA = Latvia; LTU = Lithuania; MDA = Moldova; POL = Poland; ROM = Romania; SVK = Slovak Republic; SVN = Slovenia; UKR = Ukraine.

crisis. *New structural economics* refers to the government's working with the market to ensure a country's comparative advantage. Furthermore, a number of Asian economies—Japan, the Republic of Korea, and Taiwan, China—have been successful economically through encouraging government intervention in industry and technology. Governments intervene in the economy in a number of ways:

- *To protect infant industries.* In such cases, the "first mover" has to take enormous risks, has high unit costs that lead to early losses, and has to learn by engaging in new economic activities.
- *To manage and harness technology spillovers.* As the firm becomes established and continues to grow, it is likely to create externalities or spillover effects for the rest of the industry or sector. Increasing returns to scale generate positive welfare effects for society. Harrison and Rodriguez-Clare (2009, 1) advocate tax breaks for foreign direct investment (FDI) to encourage knowledge spillovers.
- *To protect and assist informational spillovers.* Government may intervene to protect the first mover in situations where information on the industry is limited and involves large sunk costs for early learning.
- *To help the firm avoid coordination failures.* Government may provide early investments in areas where coordination failures in, for example, training, education, and infrastructure may dissuade private sector investment.
- *To ameliorate capital market failures.* Such failures can occur when even a feasible and viable new firm may not get the appropriate funding because venture capital and other financing mechanisms are not available in the country.

Table 2.2 provides examples of government intervention in a number of developing economies, spanning Africa, Asia, and Latin America.

Industrial policy has been successful in a number of countries, and East Asian countries are prime examples of successful government-led structural transformation. Other examples of industrial policy are found in Brazil and the West, for example, the support of information technology and defense industries in the United States (Wade 2011). Notwithstanding government attempts to boost economic growth in many cases such intervention has failed and proved costly for the host country. Krueger (1974) writes of the rent-seeking economy and the extraction of rents facilitated by governments that pursue their own agenda. Adverse impacts of government failure in developing countries have led to stalled

Table 2.2 Examples of Government Intervention to Support Globalization and Harness the Benefits of Employment and Growth

Instrument	Explanation	Countries or economies that have used this instrument
Tariffs	Tax or duties imposed on imports	Brazil, India, Korea, Malaysia, Russia, and Thailand
Subsidies	Financial assistance paid to an industry or sector	Japan, Korea, Malta, and Russia
Tax exemptions or credits	"Fiscal incentives" such as sector-specific levels of tax allowances on capital investment	Japan, Korea, Malta, Malaysia, Singapore, and Taiwan, China
Import licenses	A document determining the maximum volume of imports of a certain good into a country	Indonesia and Thailand
Domestic production quotas	Setting a minimum proportion of goods or components to be produced by the domestic market	Indonesia and Thailand
Export-dependent financial support	Continued favorable conditions dependent on a firm's export of a certain fraction of its goods	Korea
Public research institutions	Support investment in R&D to promote technological development	China, Singapore, and Taiwan, China
Investments in dedicated infrastructure	Facilitating the expansion of certain industries indirectly, through the promotion of investment in related infrastructure	Botswana, Brazil, and Oman
Investment in human capital	Funding and subsidizing education and training at various levels can facilitate the development of certain sectors	Singapore; China; Hong Kong, China; and Soviet Union

Source: OECD 2010.

economic diversification, private capital flight, and high debt and debt burdens. Highly selective and targeted intervention may prove effective, but only when government has good intentions. Furthermore, too much intervention is counterproductive. For example, figure 2.8 shows that excessive market regulation hurts job creation.

Globalization[11]

Globalization is associated positively with economic growth. Growth benefits from the technological advances and the spread of innovation in an integrated world economy. Economies that have embraced openness have been successful in sustaining growth and achieving economic development. While globalization creates jobs, it can also destroy jobs. The short- to medium-term effects of globalization depend largely on the country context as defined by its labor market institutions, capital markets, and social policies. Harnessing the positive benefits of globalization relies on a national policy agenda that includes economic, labor market, education, and social policies (OECD 2010, 5).

Figure 2.8   Effect of Excessive Market Regulation on Job Creation in Selected Countries in Central and Eastern Europe, 2003

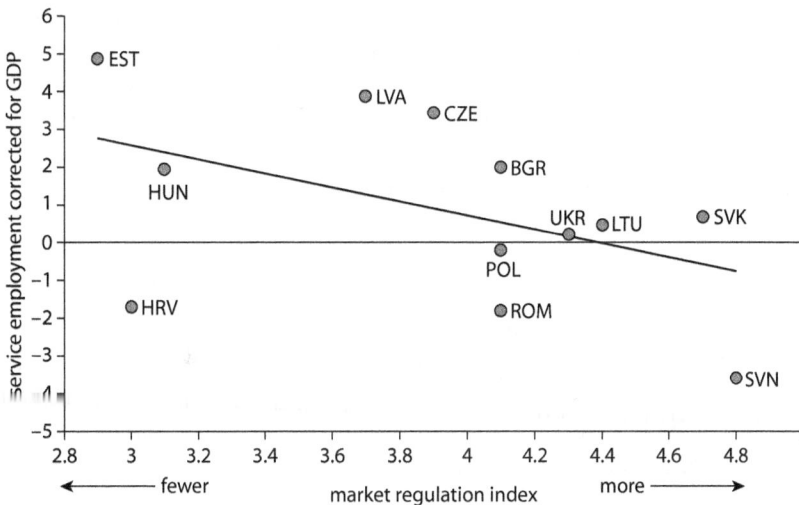

Source: Rutkowski and Scarpetta 2005, 171.
Note: BGR = Bulgaria; CZE = Czech Republic; EST = Estonia; HRV = Bosnia and Herzegovina; HUN = Hungary; LVA = Latvia; LTU = Lithuania; POL = Poland; ROM = Romania; SVK = Slovak Republic; SVN = Slovenia; UKR = Ukraine.

Trade liberalization may affect the employment rate, the wage rate, or both. The links between trade liberalization and employment are not straightforward: jobs are both created and destroyed, especially in the short to medium term. The long-run picture is more favorable. OECD (2010)[12] notes the rise in employment after a protracted period of trade liberalization.[13]

Trade liberalization affects labor within an industry as the more productive, export-oriented firms typically employ higher-skilled individuals and pay higher wages. Labor is reallocated within industries. The ease with which this adjustment happens depends on the country context, as noted above, and complementary policies in these areas. The difference between the wages paid by the firms in the export sector and those in the nonexport sector is known as the export wage premium. A number of studies cited in OECD (2010, 9)[14] document the existence of this premium in both developed and developing countries. In Western Europe, exporting firms tend to pay wages that are 10–20 percent higher than wages paid in nonexporting firms (OECD 2010, 9).

Strengthening Labor Markets

Strengthening labor markets to promote employment creation was the focus of the recent ILO-IMF report on meeting the challenges of growth, employment, and social cohesion. The large increase in unemployment and the uneven pattern of globalization have focused attention on labor market institutions and policies to generate sustainable employment. Sustainable employment will be achieved only through macroeconomic and employment policies working together. This section examines the three interconnected priorities identified by the report for strengthening labor market institutions:

- Improving the mechanisms for wage determination to raise living standards for all working families
- Promoting productivity growth by supporting worker mobility and micro and small business development
- Narrowing income inequalities through more inclusive labor markets and stronger social protection (ILO-IMF 2010, 74)

Globalization and technological advances have changed the world of work while increasing the scope for inefficiencies and inequities. Achieving equity and efficiency is a challenge for labor market institutions that are slow to adjust. Nevertheless, significant deregulation of labor markets took place in many countries, with mixed results. According to the ILO-IMF report, "In too many countries, inequalities have widened, good jobs were not generated in sufficient quantity to meet society's needs, and problems of unemployment, underemployment and poverty persisted" (2010, 74). The Declaration of Philadelphia[15] calls for just wages to provide an adequate standard of living for all.

The ILO-IMF (2010) report recommends the following:

- Establishing a legal minimum wage with several specific aims:
  - Avoiding long periods without adjustments.
  - Avoiding large and abrupt upward movements.
  - Setting a wage level or levels with the close engagement of employers and unions to reach a well-balanced conclusion.
  - Providing the wage-setting body with adequate information and research.
  - Keeping the system manageable and simple, because multiple tiers of minimum wage rates do not yield better results.
  - Ensuring well-targeted compliance measures to ensure that legally binding minimum wages are applied in practice.
- Giving greater support to collective bargaining, including through strengthening coordinating mechanisms at the national level to connect to decentralized determination of wages and conditions:
  - Tripartite institutions involving members of the cabinet and high-level representatives of the social partners (trade unions and employer organizations) have proved effective for collective bargaining.
  - Tripartite negotiations work best when there is a comprehensive agenda with scope for trade-offs and compromises.
  - Tripartite negotiations should be cognizant of vulnerable workers and develop policies that protect and improve their situation.
  - The parties need to commit to a long-term investment in the dialogue process (ILO-IMF, 2010, 78–79).

Voluntary mobility is good for productivity. The labor market is in a constant state of flux as new jobs are created, old ones disappear, and individuals move from one job to another. Such movements are good for the macroeconomy, assuming, of course, that movement is voluntary and that a good job match between employer and employee has been found that facilitates a long-term, stable relationship in which workers can develop their skills. However, successful matchups are not always the case, and "much of the movement in the labor market consists of temporary work-ers finding new short-term jobs when the old ones end" (ILO-IMF 2010, 80). The challenge for policy is to create an environment that supports mobility to find job matches and that provides incentives for both parties to invest in a long-term relationship. The ILO-IMF report calls for employment protection legislation that will support labor mobility as well as encourage employment stability. It also advocates boosting train-ing and skills development by engaging employers and workers in deci-sions about training provisions, keeping training relevant, making opportunities accessible to men and women, and ensuring a close connec-tion between training policies and employment policies.

Small businesses are big employers, accounting, for example, for 65.5 percent of employment in Japan and 67.8 percent in Turkey (ILO-IMF 2010, 82). They represent a critical source of dynamism and innovation in an economy but are also vulnerable to economic downturns and to the investment climate as noted earlier. Policies that support access to finance, sector-specific tax incentives, eligibility to bid for public procurement contracts, support services for start-ups, market development training, and job creation and retention ensure that small business can have mac-roeconomic benefits for the whole economy.

Measures that create inclusive labor markets and extend social protec-tion represent investments in future productivity. Such measures empower workers. The ILO-IMF report (2010) suggests three ways to support these measures:

- Strengthening public and private employment services
  - Job subsidies can play a role in hiring workers who might not other-wise be hired. Good program design that targets disadvantaged groups is key to their success.
  - The "make-work-pay" measures such as the working tax credit pro-gram in the United Kingdom and the earned income tax credit in the United States are deemed effective.
- Targeting employment programs to disadvantaged communities
  - Public employment programs have proved effective when the intended beneficiaries have been reached.
- Extending social protection coverage
  - Establishing a social protection floor is increasingly being seen as a key growth and development objective, particularly for vulnerable groups. Such a floor would ensure that individuals everywhere—in both developing and developed economies—have sufficient means (through

transfers, services, and facilities) to realize basic fundamental rights (housing, sanitation, water, food, health care, and education).

∘ There is a positive correlation between social security expenditures per capita and productivity and reduction of poverty rates for developed economies, with recent studies suggesting the effects are even higher in developing economies (ILO-IMF 2010, 86).

∘ Unemployment benefits smooth consumption and income inequality, maintaining aggregate demand and contributing to economy-wide productivity during an economic downturn.

Conclusion

This chapter examined the issues surrounding job creation by considering a number of job creation channels. A stable, growing economy is critical for job creation. The recent global financial crisis dealt a severe blow to the macroeconomy, in developing and developed countries. It is important to get the macroeconomy back on track so that job creation goals continue to occupy policy makers at the national and international levels. Providing support for aggregate demand through accommodative monetary and fiscal policies will continue through 2011, as well as the pursuit of policies for easing the pain of workers and firms through employment and job subsidies. The second channel of job creation considered was investment. The investment climate affecting the firm was examined, including the risks, costs, and barriers to competition facing the firm. The Investment Climate Survey and the Doing Business Project provided information and data on the factors affecting the investment climate. Mention was made of globalization and its impact on job creation and in particular its effect on wages and employment. The chapter concludes with a discussion of how labor markets can be strengthened to meet the challenges of economic growth, employment creation, and social cohesion. The challenges of globalization and technological change were noted in outlining a role for policy in providing a just wage and more productive jobs for all.

Notes

1. Jobs are created at the level of the firm, and entrepreneurship is examined in detail in chapter 5.

2. Living on less than $1.25 per day.

3. The Investment Climate Survey covers more than 26,000 formal firms in 53 developing countries (Smith and Hallward-Driemeier 2005, 41).

4. The first report was published in 2003. The Doing Business Project covers more than 140 countries.

5. Information on the time it takes to register a business, the laws surrounding contract enforcement, and labor regulation are some of the issues covered in the report.

6. Smith and Hallward-Driemeier (2005, 41) note that "the costs associated with unreliable electricity supply alone amount to over 10 percent of sales in Eritrea, India, and Kenya, while the costs of crime exceed 10 percent of sales in Armenia, Azerbaijan, and Peru. Bribes average more than 6 percent of sales in Algeria, Cambodia, and Nicaragua."

7. The exceptional case of Lithuania may be due to changes in methodology and data sources before and after the transition (Rutkowski and Scarpetta 2005, 191).

8. "Indeed, Romania scores last in the ranking of the access-to-finance index because of its very high real interest rates, high collateral requirements, and above all, lack of protection to creditors" (Rutkowski and Scarpetta 2005, 170).

9. "By itself, access to finance explains about 40 percent of the whole increase in private sector employment predicted by the regression model" (Rutkowski and Scarpetta 2005, 170).

10. Greater government intervention is generating press and gaining attention. The opinions of Justin Lin, World Bank chief economist, who favors interventionist industrial policies by developing-country governments to augment global investment, represents a new advance in thinking on development.

11. This topic is examined in greater detail in chapter 6.

12. OECD (2010) cites Felbermayr, Prat, and Schmerer (2009); Dutt, Mitra, and Rajman (2009); and Hoekman and Winters (2007).

13. Dutt, Mitra, and Ranjan (2009) suggest that unemployment falls by 3.6 percent three years after liberalization.

14. See Beaulieu, Dehejia, and Zakhilwal (2004); Klein, Moser, and Urban (2010); and Riker (2010). For developing countries see Brambilla, Carneiro, Lederman, and Porto (2010); Green, Dickerson, and Arbache (2001); and Owen and Yu (2008).

15. The Declaration of Philadelphia was adopted in 1944 by the International Labour Organization and redefined the aims and purpose of the Organization: "The Declaration embodies the following principles: (1) Labour is not a commodity. (2) Freedom of expression and of association are essential to sustained progress. (3) Poverty anywhere constitutes a danger to prosperity everywhere. (4) All human beings, irrespective of race, creed or sex, have the right to pursue both their material well-being and their spiritual development in

conditions of freedom and dignity, of economic security and equal opportunity." http://www.ilo.org/public/english/bureau/inf/download/brochure/pdf/page5.pdf.

References

Beaulieu, Eugene, Vivek Dehejia, and Hazrat-Omar Zakhilwal. 2004. "International Trade, Labour Turnover, and the Wage Premium: Testing the Bhagwati-Dehejia Hypothesis for Canada," CESifo Working Paper Series 1149, CESifo Group, Munich.

Brambilla, Irene, Rafael Dix Carneiro, Daniel Lederman, and Guido Porto. 2010. "Skills, Exports, and the Wages of Five Million Latin American Workers." World Bank Policy Research Working Paper 5246. Washington, D.C.: World Bank.

Dutt, P., D. Mitra, and P. Ranjan. 2009. "International Trade and Unemployment: Theory and Cross-National Evidence." *Journal of International Economics* 78 (1).

Elder, S. 2010. "Youth for Hire." *Finance and Development* 47 (4): 26–27.

Felbermayr, G., J. Prat, and H. J. Schmerer. 2009. "Trade and Unemployment: What Do the Data Say?" IZA Discussion Paper 4184. Institute for the Study of Labor, Bonn, Germany.

Green, F., A. Dickerson, and J. S. Arbache. 2001. "A Picture of Wage Inequality and the Allocation of Labor through a Period of Trade Liberalisation: The Case of Brazil." *World Development* 29: 1923–39.

Harrison, Ann E., and Andres Rodriguez-Clare. 2009. "Trade, Foreign Investment, and Industrial Policy for Developing Countries." Working Paper 15261. National Bureau of Economic Research, Cambridge, MA.

Hoekman, B., and L. A. Winters. 2007. "Trade and Employment: Stylized Facts and Research Findings." In *Policy Matters: Economic and Social Policies to Sustain Equitable Development*, ed. A. Ocampo, K. S. Jomo, and S. Khan, 76–105. London and Opus, New Delhi: Zed Books.

ILO (International Labour Organization)-IMF (International Monetary Fund). 2010. "The Challenges of Growth, Employment and Social Cohesion." Discussion document prepared for the joint ILO-IMF conference in cooperation with the office of the Prime Minister of Norway, http://www.osloconference2010.org/discussionpaper.pdf.

IMF. (International Monetary Fund). 2008. "Globalization: A Brief Overview," http://www.imf.org/external/np/exr/ib/2008/053008.htm.

Klein, Michael W., Christoph Moser, and Dieter M. Urban, 2010. "The Contribution of Trade to Wage Inequality: The Role of Skill, Gender, and

Nationality." NBER Working Paper 15985, National Bureau of Economic Research, Inc., Cambridge, MA.

Krueger, A. 1974. "The Political Economy of the Rent Seeking Society." *American Economic Review* 64 (3): 291–303.

OECD (Organisation for Economic Co-operation and Development). 2010. "Seizing the Benefits of Trade for Employment and Growth," http://www .oecd.org/dataoecd/61/57/46353240.pdf.

Owen, Ann L., and Bing Y. Yu. 2008. "Regional Differences in Wage Inequality across Industries in China." *Applied Economics Letters* 15 (2).

Riker, David. 2010. "Do Jobs in Export Industries Still Pay More? And Why?" *Manufacturing and Services Economics Brief*, July.

Rutkowski, J. J., and S. Scarpetta. 2005. *Enhancing Job Opportunities: Eastern Europe and the Former Soviet Union*. Washington, DC: World Bank.

Smith, W., and M. Hallward-Driemeier. 2005. "Understanding the Investment Climate." *Finance and Development* (March): 41–43.

Wade, R. 2011. "Why Justin Lin's Door-Opening Argument Matters for Development Economics." *Global Policy* 2 (1):115–16.

World Bank. 2004. *A Better Investment Climate for Everyone: World Development Report, 2005*. Washington, DC: World Bank.

CHAPTER 3

Labor Market Policies

The chapter examines labor market policies in developing economies. A move from job protection to worker protection has informed labor market policy, particularly in developed countries. Extending this approach to developing economies is difficult, not least because of the large informal labor market that exists there. Labor market institutions are also weak in developing countries, making it difficult to implement policies.

Labor market policies and institutions represent one of the five MILES Framework factors developed by the World Bank for the analysis of the main factors affecting employment. The framework, which brings together the factors affecting labor demand and labor supply, identifies the constraints that limit the creation of more and better jobs and helps prioritize policies. Following a brief introduction to the MILES Framework, the chapter examines the degree of informal labor markets in developing countries. This analysis provides a context for the subsequent discussion of labor market policies in developing economies. The discussion focuses on the issues involved in moving from job to worker protection.

The MILES Framework

The MILES Framework is an acronym summarizing five factors determining employment performance that arise from the interaction of labor demand and supply. MILES refers to macroeconomic performance, investment climate, labor market policies and institutions, education and skills, and social protection for workers (see table 3.1). Macroeconomic performance and the investment climate, along with labor market institutions, determine labor demand, while labor market policies and institutions, education and skills, and social protection are the factors determining labor supply.

Table 3.1 highlights the conditions for employment performance under the MILES Framework. The macroeconomic conditions refer to factors conducive to economic growth and stability. Examples include low inflation and low interest rates. The investment climate benefits from an environment favorable to private sector investment in which the regulatory environment is fair and balanced, the government is transparent in its dealings, taxes support business creation and development, adequate financing exists for entrepreneurship, infrastructure is developed, and the judiciary is fair and effective. Labor market policies and institutions aim to promote an adaptable labor market in which employers have incentives to hire workers and employees have incentives and the skills to take up employment. Education and skills are needed to respond to the demand for labor and training, and lifelong learning is required to meet the changing demands for labor in a high-growth, competitive economy. Social protection through social risk management programs and social insurance

Table 3.1   The MILES Framework

Factors affecting employment performance	*Policy issues*
Macroeconomic conditions	Conditions for growth
	Macroeconomic stability
Investment climate	Regulatory environment
	Government transparency
	Taxes
	Financing
	Infrastructure
	Legal environment
Labor market policies and institutions	Labor market regulation
	Wage setting
	Nonwage costs
Education and skills	Basic education
	Higher education
	Training and lifelong learning
Social protection	Social risk management programs
	Social insurance

Source: World Bank 2008.

ensures that adequate social safety nets exist, especially for those workers willing to work.

The Informal Labor Market

The existence of the informal labor market hampers the effect of labor market policies. It is also likely to coexist with a weak institutional capacity to implement labor market reforms or policies. Informal labor markets are a large part of the discourse on developing economies; yet there is no one definition that embraces the theoretical, empirical, or policy aspects of this concept. According to Sanchez-Puerta (2010, 23), "The concept of the informal labor market relates to the notion of non-participation in tax systems, in social security systems, and meeting regulatory requirements." Participation in the informal labor market is higher among microentrepreneurs, the self-employed, and workers employed in informal sector firms or informal workers within registered firms (Betcherman 2002).

There are a number of dimensions to the informal labor market discussed in the literature.[1] Among these are the informal labor market's contribution to (1) employment, (2) output, (3) type of activity and enterprise, (4) type of employment skills and human capital, (5) earnings, (6) access to capital and credit, (7) duality within the informal sector, (8) legality, (9) poverty, and (10) female workers (Sanchez-Puerta 2010, 24). The number of dimensions ascribed to the informal labor market, definitional issues, and data limitations render its measurement difficult. Henley, Arabsheibani, and Carneiro (2006) cited in Sanchez-Puerta (2010) considered three different definitions of informality using data from Brazil for 1992–2001. Definitions of informality were based on employment contract registration, social security protection, and characteristics of employer and employment. The results indicated that around 64 percent of the economically active population was informal according to one definition, whereas 40 percent was considered informal according to all three definitions. The authors found a close correspondence between an employment contract and not contributing to a social security scheme, although a significant number of the economically active were classified as informal according to the nature of their employment or employer even when they were contributing to social security (Sanchez-Puerta 2010, 24).

The informal labor market accounts for approximately 60–80 percent of total nonagricultural employment in Sub-Saharan Africa, with similarly large proportions in South and Southeast Asia. The informal labor market in Latin America and North Africa is smaller, accounting for between 30 and 60 percent of total nonagricultural employment, while the informal sector in Central Europe and East Asia accounts for between 5 and 20 percent[2] (Sanchez-Puerta 2010, 24). And in his study of the contribution of output to the informal sector, Charmes (2000) determined that it contributed between 20 and 50 percent of nonagricultural gross domestic product in Sub-Saharan Africa (excluding South Africa), with similar proportions for South and Southeast Asia and a number of countries in Latin America.

In 2010, the International Labour Organization sought to measure informal activity by concentrating on "vulnerable employment." Vulnerable employment is one of the official employment indicators of the Millennium Development Goals. It refers to the sum of own-account workers and unpaid family workers. Vulnerable workers "typically lack social protection and social dialogue mechanisms and are often characterized by low pay and difficult working conditions in which workers' fundamental rights may be undermined" (ILO 2011, 22).[3] Figure 3.1 shows the global trends in vulnerable employment for 1999–2009.

Figure 3.1   Global Trends in Vulnerable Employment, 1999–2009

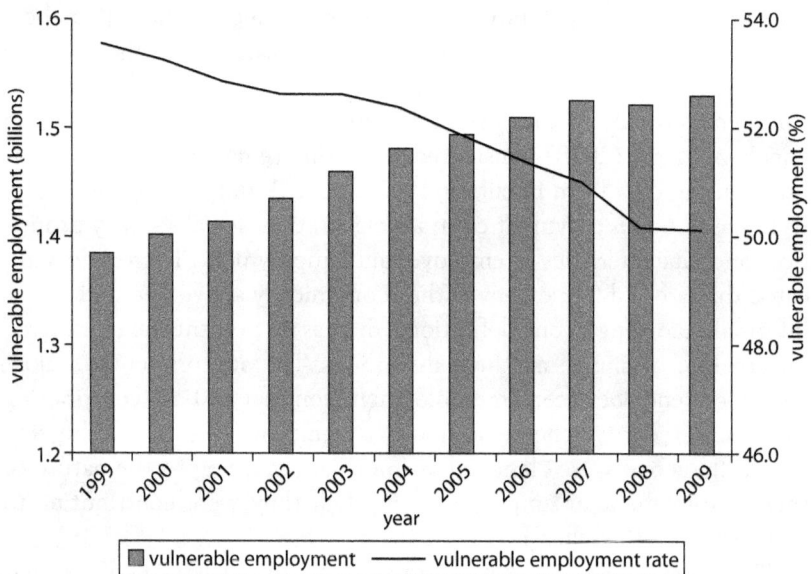

Source: ILO 2011, 23.
Note: 2009 is a preliminary estimate.

Roughly 1.53 billion workers were estimated to be in vulnerable employment in 2009, an increase of more than 146 million since 1999. These figures correspond to a global vulnerable employment rate of 50.1 percent. That rate declined annually from close to 54 percent in 1999 to just over 50 percent in 2008 and maintained that rate in 2009. The financial crisis of 2008 witnessed a large number of workers moving into the informal labor markets as recessions hit, undoing the significant gains made in the years preceding the crisis.

Table 3.2 examines the regional vulnerable employment rates for various years between 1998 and 2009. As noted above, the vulnerable employment rate for the world declined from a rate of about 54 percent in 1998 to about 50 percent in 2009. Most regions experienced a decline after 1998, although the decline for Southeast Asia and the Pacific and for South Asia began in 2000. Among the regions, the rate of vulnerable employment in 2009 was highest in South Asia (78.5 percent), Sub-Saharan Africa (75.8 percent), and Southeast Asia and the Pacific (61.8 percent). It was lowest among the developed economies and European Union (EU) (9.7 percent), with the rate in Latin America and the Caribbean and the Middle East roughly the same at around 32 percent. The vulnerable employment rate increased in Latin America and the Caribbean in 2009, and the Middle East region and Sub-Saharan Africa also showed an increase from the rate in 2008.

Table 3.2   World and Regional Rates of Vulnerable Employment, Various Years, 1998–2009

	1998	1999	2000	2005	2006	2007	2008	2009
World	53.7	53.5	53.3	51.9	51.4	51.0	50.2	50.1
Developed economies and European Union	11.3	11.1	10.8	10.3	10.0	9.9	9.7	9.7
Central and southeastern Europe (non-EU) and CIS	24.1	26.7	25.6	22.8	21.9	20.7	20.4	20.0
East Asia	61.4	60.2	59.1	55.8	55.2	54.5	52.2	50.8
Southeast Asia and the Pacific	63.8	66.2	65.5	62.6	62.3	62.0	62.5	61.8
South Asia	81.9	81.1	82.1	80.5	80.2	79.9	78.9	78.5
Latin America and the Caribbean	35.7	36.1	35.8	33.8	32.7	32.3	31.8	32.2
Middle East	36.8	36.0	35.7	33.9	33.7	33.3	32.9	32.7
North Africa	43.7	42.1	42.4	42.6	41.1	41.2	40.2	40.4
Sub-Saharan Africa	80.5	79.9	79.5	77.1	76.6	76.0	75.3	75.8

Source: ILO 2011, 69.

Table 3.3 examines the number of workers in vulnerable employ-ment for various years between 1998 and 2009. Between 2008 and 2009, the number of workers in vulnerable employment is estimated to have increased by 8.5 million workers (1.7 percent) in South Asia, by 7.4 million workers in Sub-Saharan Africa, and by 1.5 million in Latin America and the Caribbean. Minor increases also occurred in Southeast Asia and the Pacific, North Africa, and the Middle East (ILO 2011, 21).

Gender differences in the number of workers in vulnerable employ-ment are stark in many regions, especially in North Africa and the Middle East where the percentage difference between males and females was over 21 percentage points and over 14 percentage points, respectively, in 2009. The gender difference in Sub-Saharan Africa was also over 14 percentage points in 2009. Indeed, all regions, except the developed economies and the European Union, Central and Southeastern Europe (non-EU), and the Russian Federation show a higher vulnerable employment rate among women than among men (see table 3.4).

The North Africa region stands out as one in which the vulnerable employment rate among women has actually increased over the study period, from 55.4 percent in 1998 to 56.7 percent in 2009, with the high-est rate occurring in 2007 (59.3 percent). Thus, since the financial crisis, female vulnerable employment in North Africa has actually improved. The largest percentage-point declines in female vulnerable employment over the study period took place in Central and Southeastern Europe (non-EU), Russia, and the Middle East. In those locations, women may have found work in the formal labor market, returned to or entered fur-ther education, or register as unemployed.

Since the financial crisis in 2008, male vulnerable employment fared worse in the Middle East, North Africa, and Sub-Saharan Africa. The percentage-point differences between 2008 and 2009 for female vulnerable employment in these regions were –0.5, –1.5, and station-ary, respectively, whereas the percentage-point differences for men were +0.2, +0.8, and +1.0, respectively. Both males and females fared worse in vulnerable employment in Latin America and the Caribbean, where the percentage-point differences were 0.3 and 0.6, respectively. In fact, women fared worst in Latin America and the Caribbean of all other regions in a comparison of vulnerable employment shares in 2008 with those in 2009 (see table 3.4).

Vulnerable employment is a large proportion of the economy's employment in South Asia, Sub-Saharan Africa, and Southeast Asia and

Table 3.3   Number of Workers in Vulnerable Employment, Various Years, 1998–2009
(millions)

	1998	1999	2000	2005	2006	2007	2008	2009
World	1,364.4	1,382.3	1,399.4	1,489.7	1,505.3	1,521.6	1,519.3	1,528.2
Developed economies and European Union	49.5	49.1	48.5	47.6	47.1	47.2	46.5	45.6
Central and southeastern Europe (non-EU) and CIS	34.7	38.5	37.5	35.2	34.4	33.1	33.1	32.1
East Asia	450.3	445.2	443.1	444.4	441.8	439.6	421.7	413.2
Southeast Asia and the Pacific	145.2	155.3	156.8	162.7	165.0	168.3	172.9	173.7
South Asia	404.7	408.2	421.1	473.0	484.0	493.6	500.2	508.7
Latin America and the Caribbean	70.6	72.9	73.8	79.0	78.8	79.5	80.1	81.6
Middle East	16.0	16.4	16.9	19.0	19.5	19.9	20.0	20.5
North Africa	20.9	20.7	21.2	25.2	25.2	25.9	26.1	26.8
Sub-Saharan Africa	172.5	176.0	180.4	203.6	209.5	214.5	218.8	226.2

Source: ILO 2011, 70.

Table 3.4 Vulnerable Employment Rate by Sex, Various Years, 1998–2009
(percent)

	1998		1999		2000		2005		2006		2007		2008		2009	
	Males	Females	Males	Females	Males	Females	Males	Females	Males	Females	Males	Females	Males	Females	Males	Females
World	52.0	56.3	51.8	56.1	51.8	55.5	50.5	54.0	50.0	53.5	49.5	53.2	48.9	52.1	48.9	51.8
Developed economies and European Union	11.8	10.7	11.7	10.3	11.4	10.1	11.3	9.1	11.0	8.8	10.9	8.6	10.7	8.4	10.8	8.4
Central and southeastern Europe (non-EU) and CIS	24.7	23.4	26.7	26.7	25.8	25.4	23.3	22.1	22.4	21.3	20.9	20.4	20.6	20.2	20.2	19.8
East Asia	56.7	67.1	55.7	65.7	54.7	64.4	51.9	60.6	51.3	59.9	50.6	59.2	48.9	56.2	47.8	54.6
Southeast Asia and the Pacific	60.4	68.6	62.5	71.3	61.8	70.6	59.6	67.0	59.3	66.5	58.7	66.6	59.7	66.4	58.9	65.7
South Asia	79.0	89.2	78.1	88.5	79.9	87.6	78.0	86.5	77.5	86.3	77.2	86.1	76.2	85.0	75.8	84.5
Latin America and the Caribbean	35.0	37.0	35.4	37.3	35.3	36.5	33.5	34.3	32.6	33.0	31.8	33.0	31.3	32.6	31.6	33.2
Middle East	33.6	49.9	32.4	50.8	31.8	51.6	30.2	48.0	30.1	46.8	29.8	46.5	29.8	44.2	29.6	43.7
North Africa	40.1	55.4	38.7	52.9	38.2	56.0	37.0	59.7	35.4	58.3	35.1	59.3	34.1	58.2	34.9	56.7
Sub-Saharan Africa	75.5	87.3	74.5	87.1	74.0	86.9	70.1	86.2	69.6	85.6	69.2	84.9	68.5	84.0	69.5	84.0

Source: ILO 2011, 69.

the Pacific regions. The downward trend in vulnerable employment, however, has been knocked off course in the wake of the financial crisis, with Latin America and the Caribbean faring worst, especially among women. Gender differences in vulnerable employment are evident across all developing regions, with stark differences in North Africa, the Middle East, and South Asia.

Sanchez-Puerta (2010) examines the reasons why the informal labor market has not declined over time as policy makers and economists had expected. Citing Betcherman (2002), Sanchez-Puerta (2010, 30) lists the following reasons for the incorrect prediction:

- *The "no-growth" hypothesis.* The modern industrial and formal sector has not grown fast enough to absorb the growing labor force and hence the informal sector has continued to expand.
- *The "jobless growth" hypothesis.* The technology used in the formal sector has not been conducive to the further absorption of labor into that sector.
- *The "growth from below" hypothesis.* Small and microenterprises themselves represent a vibrant sector, and some entrepreneurs may choose to operate in that sector.
- *The "regulatory disincentive" hypothesis.* Employers, and sometimes workers, choose the informal sector because it is too costly to operate in the formal sector.

Moreover, the World Bank (2006) noted that jobs shifted from formal to informal in Europe and Central Asia, including an increase in self-employment. While any one or a combination of these factors may account for continuance and expansion of the informal labor market, the situation in each country will be different, depending on its labor market institutions. Any policy promoting employment creation in the formal sector needs to be mindful of the country context.

Moving from Job to Worker Protection

Moving from job to worker protection involves a move from policies that support employment protection toward policies that provide income and nonincome support through passive and active labor market policies (ALMPs) to workers who are laid off or unemployed. The economic effects of employment protection legislation (EPL)—the rules relating to hiring and firing—can be substantial. Sanchez-Puerta (2010) identifies four ways in which the effects of EPL affect labor market outcomes:

- *Labor market dynamics.* EPL affects job tenure in situations in which strong job security leads to a classic insider-outsider problem. Insiders hold onto their jobs in upturns and downturns, and hiring opportunities for outsiders are limited. Thus, labor market turnover is stultified. As Sanchez-Puerta (2010) notes, "Duration of unemployment (and employment) is expected to be positively correlated to the degree of employment protection" (3).
- *Employment levels.* The average level of employment through the business cycle is more ambiguous with EPL. Whether employment rates increase or decrease depends on hiring and firing decisions that, in turn, depend upon labor elasticity of demand, decisions made by the employer on future hiring costs, and assumptions about the longevity of labor demand shocks.
- *Composition of employment.* EPL may encourage firms to move activities to the informal sector.
- *Productivity growth.* The theoretical literature suggests a decline in average productivity with stringent EPL. Costly EPL may slow down the adoption of new technologies.

There are a number of issues to examine in considering the empirical effects of EPL on labor market outcomes. First, EPL is relevant only in the formal labor market and thus has limited relevance in many developing countries, given the significant presence of informal labor as outlined earlier. Second, measuring the effect of EPL on labor market outcomes is problematic. It is difficult to create standardized measures of EPL. It is also difficult to measure enforcement of EPL. These measurement problems make it difficult to compare cross-country results.[4] Third, labor market regulations change infrequently and are applied at the national level to all workers, making it difficult to ascertain the effects across areas and sectors. Sanchez-Puerta (2010) reviews a number of studies, and the results from a selected few are shown in table 3.5.

Further stylized facts about the effect of EPL on economic activity and labor market outcomes are noted by Sanchez-Puerta (2010) as follows:

- Employment promotion legislation reduces turnover.[5]
- The effect of employment protection regulations on employment and unemployment is not conclusive for some studies,[6] while others suggest a negative relationship.[7]

Table 3.5 Measuring the Impact of Employment Protection Legislation

Study	Objective	Sample	Method	Results
Micco and Pagés (2006)	Estimate economic effects of EPL	Developed and developing countries	Difference-in-difference	1. EPL reduces job flows, particularly in (a) volatile sectors and (b) countries with better law enforcement. 2. By reducing industry size, EPL is likely to reduces (aggregate): (a) firm entry, (b) employment, and (c) value-added.
Haltiwanger, Scarpetta, and Schweiger (2006)	Effect of EPL on job turnover	Firm-level data for 16 industrial and emerging economies	Difference-in-difference	1. Stringent EPL reduces job turnover, especially in industries that require more frequent labor adjustment. 2. EPL regulations distort the patterns of industry size and flows.
Petrin and Sivadasan (2006)	Effect of EPL on manufacturing firms	Census data on Chilean manufacturing firms between 1979 and 1996	Compares outcomes between workers. Authors develop a new statistic that estimates the within-firm gap between marginal product of labor and its marginal cost (wage).	1. EPL drives a wedge between marginal revenue and marginal cost that is statistically significant for (a) white collar and (b) blue collar workers. 2. There is little positive effect on the mean and variance gap for nonlabor inputs.
Besley and Burgess (2004)	Effect of EPL on employment, productivity, and poverty	Indian manufacturing between 1958 and 1992	Develop a theoretical model linking bargaining power with economic performance	1. EPL is associated with lowered employment, investment, productivity, and output in registered manufacturing. 2. EPL is positively associated with increases in urban poverty.

Source: Compiled from Sanchez-Puerta 2010, 6–7.

- There is a positive relationship between employment protection and self-employment.[8]
- Employment protection changes the composition of employment.[9]
- Evidence on productivity is slim, particularly in developing countries.[10]
- Most developing-country studies of EPL focus on efficiency outcomes and not on equity.[11]

Sanchez-Puerta (2010) concludes her review of the theoretical and empirical literature on EPL by noting some further areas of study. In addition to improving the measurement of EPL, she suggests improving the data to facilitate deeper analysis of microdata sets and matching employer-employee comparisons under different labor practices while highlighting the subsequent effects on selectivity of workers and productivity. An enormous gap in the literature is the lack of knowledge on the political economy of labor market reforms and also on "adapting labor legislation to the feminization of the labor force" (Sanchez-Puerta 2010, 10).

On the labor supply side, organized or unionized labor is active mainly in the protected sectors of the economy, namely, the public sector, banking, and the civil service. Permanent workers in the formal sector are often covered by collective bargaining. Of course, in the informal labor market, unionized labor is nonexistent. Sanchez-Puerta (2010) recommends analyzing the effects of the interaction of EPL with labor market institutions, such as collective bargaining, on labor market outcomes.

Passive Labor Market Policies

Passive labor market policies are also known as income-support policies. Examples include unemployment insurance (UI), unemployment assistance (UA), severance pay, unemployment insurance savings accounts (UISA), and public works (PW). The aim of these policies is to smooth consumption for the individual affected by involuntary job loss and reduce income inequalities. Further benefits to society are helping the poor and long-term unemployed, promoting restructuring of enterprises, and increasing output and efficiency. Table 3.6 categorizes the types of instruments by benefit level, duration, and eligibility.

Unemployment insurance has many advantages and is widely lauded in the income protection literature (Sanchez-Puerta 2010, 12). It offers a high degree of protection to formal sector workers, contributing to consumption smoothing and macroeconomic stability. It also has

Table 3.6   Attributes of Income-Support Policies

Instrument	Benefit level	Duration	Eligibility
Unemployment insurance	Percentage of past wage, sometimes declining	Limited	1. Conditional on past contributions 2. No-fault dismissal 3. Availability and willingness to work and job search
Unemployment assistance	Topping the income to reach a specific threshold in terms of average family income	Unlimited (if self-standing) or limited (after unemployment insurance has expired)	Means tested
Severance pay	Lump-sum payment, generally based on years of service	One-time payment	Laid off workers (not for just cause)
Unemployment insurance savings accounts	Replacement rate as under unemployment insurance	Limited	Conditional on availability of funds in individual's savings account (with optional limited borrowing)
Public works	Typically set below market wage	Usually limited	Anyone (self-selection based on low wage)

Source: Compiled from Vodopivec and Raju 2004.

negative effects, chiefly prolonging unemployment. Because moral hazard and the significant information required on individuals make this a difficult program to operate in developing countries, it is primarily available only in developed economies (see table 3.7). Sanchez-Puerta (2010) reviews a number of studies of UI and concludes that "ultimately the performance of UI depends on the design of the program—and also on country-specific conditions" (14). UI systems are common in developed economies, most transition economies in Eastern Europe, and some Latin American economies.

Unemployment assistance (UA) outperforms UI in redistributing income to the poor and reaching a wider audience. It has, however, a number of weaknesses as outlined in table 3.7. Weaknesses arise from its screening of individuals based on an income or means test. UA benefits are contingent on family income and assets and so may reduce labor supply of other family members. Vodopivec and Raju (2004, 4), citing Atkinson (1995), notes that "in Western countries a third or more of potential claimants never receive means-tested benefits (the reasons being information problems, administrative complexities, and stigmatization of recipients)."

Table 3.7 Income-Support Policies, Advantages, Disadvantages, and Income Group Relevance

Instrument	Positives	Negatives	Income group suitability
Unemployment insurance	1. Enables a high degree of consumption smoothing 2. Performs well under various types of shocks 3. Acts as an automatic macroeconomic stabilizer	1. Creates reemployment disincentives and wage pressures	Developed countries
Unemployment assistance	1. Enables more effective targeting	1. May not bring savings 2. Offers a lower level of protection for high-income workers 3. Imposes larger administrative costs 4. Similar employment disincentives to UI	Countries with developed administrative capacity and small informal sector
Unemployment insurance savings accounts	1. Ameliorates moral hazard inherent in UI, improving reemployment incentives 2. May improve work incentives 3. Potential to attract informal sector workers	1. System largely untested 2. Allowing individuals to borrow from their accounts may lead to some leaving the formal sector to avoid paying debt.	Developed countries and developing countries
Severance pay[a]	Little advantage		Available in many developing and transition economies
Public works	1. Effective in reaching the poor 2. Good targeting properties 3. Substantial capacity to redistribute income from rich to poor 4. Able to attract informal sector workers 5. Provides flexible and fast response to shocks 6. Administratively less demanding than other income-support policies	1. High nonwage costs 2. Likely countercyclical pattern of funding 3. May lead to stigmatization of participants in some countries	Developing countries, particularly as a complementary program.

Source: Compiled from Vodopivec and Raju 2004.

a. Severance pay is an important program in developing and transition countries; yet there are issues with its protection and efficiency effects. Prefunding may improve the nonperformance of this program and associated labor market rigidities (Vodopivec and Raju 2004, 21).

Unemployment insurance savings accounts require individuals to save a fraction of their wages in special savings accounts. They can then draw from these accounts if they become unemployed. Any positive balances will be added to retirement benefits and negative balances forgiven upon retirement. UISAs are viewed as an improvement on UI, negating the moral hazard problem that can arise as individuals withdraw their own savings to smooth consumption. However, there are negatives as outlined in table 3.7, not least is that individuals may withdraw funds in advance, knowing that the "government will compensate for negative balances" (Sanchez-Puerta 2010, 15). UISAs are common in some Latin American economies, such as Brazil and Colombia, where they have morphed from funded severance pay systems.

Severance pay as noted in table 3.6 refers to lump-sum payments paid to individuals who have been laid off either by employers as part of firm policy or as required by governments. Severance pay is limited to formal sector workers with contracts in the private sector, and as such the proportion of workers covered by severance pay is low, particularly in developing countries.[12] Despite this factor, severance pay is the most common income-support system in developing countries, apart from low-income countries (Vodopivec and Raju 2004). Furthermore, such payments do not take into account the duration of unemployment; thus, discharged workers may not receive enough compensation for the period they are unemployed (see table 3.7). The manner in which severance pay operates, despite providing income support, has more in common with job protection than worker protection. Vodopivec and Raju (2004, 6) citing Lazear (1990) notes that "severance pay reduces both employment and labor force participation." Other evidence suggests that it reduces inflows to and outflows from unemployment.

Aimed at labor-intensive sectors, public works provide publicly funded, low-wage work to poor workers. Wages are often set below the market rate. It is the most prevalent form of income support in low-income countries, with some 80 percent of countries having public works programs. Such programs also often exist in middle- and high-income countries (Vodopivec and Raju 2004, 7). It is a flexible system, effective in reaching the poor and in attracting informal workers to the formal sector. On the negative side, Ravallion (1991, 1999) notes that high nonwage costs in low-income countries can reduce the effectiveness of the program. Workers may be stigmatized, and the countercyclical nature of such programs may make it difficult for firms to raise funding at the precise time it is needed most (see table 3.7).

Vodopivec and Raju (2002) categorizes income-support policies on labor market outcomes by efficiency effects, distributive effects, suitability to confront economic shocks, and resistance to political interference. In addition, the effects will depend on how the income-support policies interact with the labor market and labor market institutions, the administrative capacity of the country, and the size of the informal sector. Table 3.8 lists the distributive and efficiency effects of the five income-support policies under review.

For their distributive effects, public works programs are the most progressive of all income-support policies.[13] Implementation of the public works program is key to the successful targeting of the poor (Coady 2002). Unemployment assistance programs are also strongly progressive. Vodopivec and Raju (2004) note the case of Australia in particular. UA programs are fundamentally a developed-economy occurrence, given the stronger administrative capacity and smaller informal sector in developed countries. Vodopivec and Raju (2004) refer to UA's strongly progressive distributive effect in transition countries and suggest that this effect may be due to the nearly universal benefit coverage in these countries, a situation not found in developing countries. The efficiency effects of income-support policies may be summarized as follows:

- *The job search effort.* Public works show little effect; unemployment assistance shows the most.
- *Postunemployment wages.* Evidence of improved job matching based on postunemployment wages is inconclusive.
- *Equilibrium labor market outcomes.* These outcomes range from increasing unemployment where UI and UA affect job-search intensity and wage bargaining to reducing unemployment when individuals become involved in public works programs.
- *Enhancing restructuring of enterprises.* UI is an increasingly attractive income-support policy.
- *Labor supply of other family members.* Unemployment assistance creates a disincentive.
- *Encouragement to take regular jobs.* Negative effect on labor reallocation with severance pay.
- *Output and growth.* The effects of public works are negligible.

Developing economies tend to have weak social security systems (Sanchez-Puerta 2010, 11) and rely heavily on severance pay. The limitations of this policy were discussed above. In some Latin American

Table 3.8 Distributive and Efficiency Effects of Income-Support Policies

Instrument	Distributive			Efficiency		
	Poverty	Income redistribution	Labor market	Restructuring	Job search
Unemployment insurance	Mild reduction	Neutral	1. Increases unemployment 2. Slows adjustment shocks	1. Job creation hindered 2. Overall adjustment slow	1. Moral hazard 2. Inconclusive evidence on job matching
Unemployment assistance	Mild reduction	Strongly progressive[a]	Disincentive for other family members to take a job	Similar to UI	Disincentive to leave unemployment
Severance pay	Some reduction	Biased[b]	1. Reduces employment 2. Increases participation in informal sectors 3. Effects on unemployment inconclusive	1. Negative effects on labor reallocation 2. Reduction of inflow to unemployment 3. Reduction of job creation	No moral hazard
Unemployment insurance savings account	Inconclusive	Biased	1. Little effect on reducing labor demand[c] 2. Little effect on employment[c]	Conversion of severance pay into UISA increased both firing and hiring by firms[c]	No moral hazard
Public works	Strong reduction	Strongly progressive	1. Mildly reduces unemployment 2. Mildly increases employment	Negligible effects	If wages kept low, little effect on job search efforts

Source: Compiled from Vodopivec and Raju 2002.

a. Refers to Australia where UA is a primary income replacement program.

b. Refers to Peru, where the benefits were concentrated on the rich and there was higher consumption by the severance pay recipients compared to similarly employed workers.

c. Refers to Colombia.

countries, prefunding of severance pay has circumvented some of the issues. Vodopivec and Raju (2004) refer to the worse administrative capacity in developing economies and the many opportunities to work in the informal sector compared to the developed economies. They suggest that developing and transition economies choose among the income-support policies for the unemployed, paying close attention to the underlying country context—the degree of informality in the labor market and the effectiveness of the labor market institutions.[14]

Active Labor Market Policies

The effectiveness of income-support policies is enhanced when the overall labor market policy takes into account employment protection. Furthermore, income-support policies are more effective when complemented with active labor market policies. Active labor market policies include the following:

- Programs that enhance labor supply through training
- Programs that improve the functioning of the labor market through employment services
- Programs that increase labor demand through public works or subsidies (Sanchez-Puerta 2010, 17).

Training and retraining programs represent the bulk of active labor market policies, accounting for between 40 and 60 percent of expenditures on total ALMPs in most countries (Sanchez-Puerta 2010, 17, citing Betcherman, Olivas, and Dar 2004). ALMPs focus on developing human capacity with the aim of achieving a more positive and enduring employment outcome. By themselves, ALMPs cannot solve unemployment, but they do help in mitigating its effects (Spevacek 2009).

Sanchez-Puerta (2010) reviews a number of training programs that have been carried out in Latin America and the Caribbean. A sample of these studies is summarized in table 3.9.

The findings for ALMPs are mixed. Some stylized facts, based on the findings from table 3.9 above and the review of the literature carried out by Sanchez-Puerta (2010), point to several conclusions:

- The quality of the training program is critical: the higher the quality, the better the outcome.
- The majority of training programs in Latin America and the Caribbean come from private providers (Sanchez-Puerta 2010, 19). This is the

Table 3.9   Effectiveness of Training Programs in Latin America and the Caribbean

Type of active labor market policy	Country	Findings
Job training[a]	Argentina, Chile, Dominican Republic, Mexico, Panama, Peru	1. Range of employment effects from null to 10 percentage points 2. Variation of employment effects by age, gender, and region 3. Higher employment effects for women and youth 4. Positive impact in terms of the quality of job that participants get 5. Direct costs of program recovered quickly 6. Positive rates of return in relation to costs
Youth programs[b] (motivating youth and on-the-job training of young school dropouts and other vulnerable youths)	Argentina, Chile, Dominican Republic, Peru	1. Quality of program makes a difference in outcome for participants. 2. Youths in Peru had 32% higher earnings 18 months after the course[c].
In-firm training[d]	Mexico	1. Employer-provided training was more widespread among manufacturing firms over the study period, during the 1990s. 2. A higher proportion of the workforce also received training. 3. Technological change was the catalyst for training. 4. Training had large and statistically significant wage and productivity outcomes. 5. Joint-training and R&D yielded larger returns compared to investment in one or the other. 6. Training and technology investments enabled firms to improve their relative position in wage and productivity distribution.

Source: Compiled from Sanchez-Puerta 2010, 17–20.

a. Ibarraran and Rosas 2006.
b. Puerto. 2007.
c. Chong and Galdo 2006.
d. Tan and Lopez Azevedo 2003.

case especially in Chile and Uruguay, whereas firms in Belize, Ecuador, Nicaragua, and Trinidad and Tobago involve public trainers.

- Private trainers outperformed public trainers in Brazil, Colombia, and the Caribbean (Marquez 2002; Barrera and Higuera 2004). The public sector oversees enforcement of quality and monitoring of training.
- On-the-job training is more effective than classroom training (World Bank 2004; Pagés, Pierre, and Scarpetta 2009).
- The capital intensity of a firm is positively associated with the demand for training.
- Government training programs in lieu of formal education do not work; training at the firm level should enhance productivity.
- Most of the analysis of training programs is short term, generally 18 months after the program, and generally does not include an assessment of cost effectiveness (Sanchez-Puerta 2010, 19).
- Training has a positive effect on employment prospects, although participants generally do not experience an increase in wages when they return to work (Spevacek 2009, 3).
- Aggregate unemployment may remain unaffected as retrainees may displace previously employed workers (Spevacek 2009, 3).
- Data for the United States show more positive effects on adult women than on adult men (Friedlander, Greenberg, and Robins 1997; Stanley, Katz, and Krueger 1998).

Spevacek (2009, 4) reviews ALMPs for Central and Eastern Europe and Russia. The studies reviewed fell into the following categories (some studies contained more than one ALMP):

- *Self-employment and small business assistance.* This type of assistance supports the creation and advancement of self-employment activities or microenterprises by providing counseling services, including how to write and use a business plan, short-term entrepreneurial training, and (often) financial assistance (9 studies).
- *Employment services.* This type of assistance includes job counseling, placement services, relocation assistance, and the like (12 studies).
- *Skills training.* Skills training, a traditional means of solving skill mismatch in the labor market, includes on-the-job and classroom methods (14 studies).
- *Wage and employment subsidies.* These subsidies are provided to firms in the private or public sector upon hiring an unemployed person; they are typically larger the longer the person is employed with the firm (8 studies).

- *Public employment.* Jobs created by government (usually municipalities) are often targeted at long-term unemployed. Most are in construction and maintenance (public buildings, parks, and the like) and require low-level skills (17 studies).

Table 3.10 presents the findings from the review of studies in Spevacek (2009) based on the above classification. Of the nine studies that examined training for small business and self-employment, all yielded statistically significant data on getting unemployed participants back to work (see table 3.10). The data on the effect of these programs on earnings were less conclusive: the Romanian study found no effect while the Polish study indicated a positive effect (Spevacek 2009, 10).

Nine of the 12 studies examining the effect of employment services for the unemployed found a positive impact. Employment services are a cost-effective instrument of ALMP and generally improve the match between workers and jobs.

Table 3.10 Studies of Active Labor Market Policies in Selected Developing Countries in Eastern and Central Europe and the Russian Federation

Country	Small business/ self-employment assistance	Employment services	Skills training	Wage subsidies	Public works
Bosnia-Herzegovina (1 study)	n.a.	PI	PI	n.a.	n.a.
Bulgaria (2 studies)	PI	PI; NPI	PI	PI	PI
Estonia (1 study)	PI	n.a.	PI	n.a.	n.a.
Hungary (2 studies)	PI	PI; NPI	PI	NPI	NPI
Kosovo (1 study)	n.a.	n.a.	PI	n.a.	n.a.
Poland (1 study)	n.a.	n.a.	PI	NPI	NPI
Romania (3 studies)	2 PIs	PI	2 PIs	PI	2 PIs; NPI
Russian Federation (3 studies)	n.a.	2 PIs; NPI	n.a.	n.a.	NPI; PI
Slovak Republic (2 studies)	PI	PI	2 PIs	2 NPIs	2 PIs
Slovenia (2 studies)	n.a.	n.a.	n.a.	n.a.	PI; NPI
Ukraine (2 studies)	n.a.	n.a.	2 PIs	n.a.	NPI; PI
Cross country (4 studies)	3 PIs	2 PIs	2 PIs	NPI; I	2 NPIs; I
Totals (24 studies)	PI 9 NPI 0	PI 9 NPI 3	PI 14 NPI 0	PI 2 NPI 5 I 1	PI 8 NPI 8 I 1

Source: Spevacek 2009, 2.

Note: Each row represents one quantitative study. One study may have both positive and nonpositive impacts for different interventions. PI = positive impact (statistically significant); NPI = nonpositive impact (statistically insignificant); I = inconclusive; n.a. = not applicable.

Skills training programs indicate a positive impact on employment for all 14 studies considered. These programs are considered to be particularly important in Central and Eastern Europe and in Russia. In particular, the large numbers of unemployed youth make this group a priority. On-the-job training and employer involvement showed a greater impact on employment (Betcherman, Olivas, and Dar 2004, 25).

Wage and employment subsidies are a short-term measure and as a stand-alone policy are out of favor. They carry deadweight loss and substitution risk, as well as the risk of pushing up wages and reducing the demand for labor. Furthermore, wage and employment subsidies do not address skills mismatches. Just two of the eight studies reviewed found a positive impact, but these were primarily in countries with high unemployment.

Public employment programs are generally not effective for employment or earnings, and Spevacek (2009, 13) notes that "across the board, studies indicate that PW programs in Central and Eastern Europe and Russia have had consistently nonpositive impacts." In the short run, however, public employment programs may be effective. For example, in regions hit hard by an economic slump or for unemployed individuals who lack the ability to secure private sector jobs, public employment programs are considered a viable temporary solution (Spevacek 2009, 14).

Most of the studies on ALMPs examine the effectiveness of these programs. This focus provides valuable information. However, for a full understanding of the benefit of these programs, an assessment of their costs and returns to the investment is critical. Few studies undertake this objective, and, of those that do, the time frame is too short. Allocating resources to ALMPs on the basis of cost effectiveness would assist governments in ascertaining which ALMP to pursue.

Conclusion

Labor market policies are part of the MILES Framework developed by the World Bank for the purpose of examining the factors affecting employment. In addition to a stable macroeconomic environment, a skilled and educated workforce, properly functioning labor market institutions, and a healthy investment climate, labor market policies are critical in promoting an adaptable labor market in which firms are interested in hiring workers and workers have the skills and training the firms require.

Labor market policies in developed economies have evolved from job protection policies to worker protection. The large informal labor market that prevails in developing economies makes it difficult to pursue these same types of policies; yet studies have shown that job protection policies can lead to lower employment, less output, and movement out of the formal sector into the informal sector.

Evidence on the size of employment in the informal labor market is considered. The informal labor market is considerable—more than 60 percent of total employment—in South Asia, Southeast Asia and the Pacific, and Sub-Saharan Africa. The text considered "vulnerable employment" as defined by the International Labour Organization in determining the size of this sector among the developed and developing economies. The downward trend in vulnerable employment among own account and self-employed workers was reversed in the wake of the global financial crisis in 2008. Women were particularly affected.

The chapter reviewed the effectiveness of employment protection legislation, passive labor market policies (such as unemployment insurance, unemployment assistance, severance pay, public works, unemployment insurance savings accounts), and active labor market policies (training and job search services in promoting employment and reducing unemployment). The country context was important in ascertaining the effectiveness of the policies and the extent to which activities were in the formal sector. One stylized conclusion is that while no one policy holds the key to a fully functioning labor market, the answer lies in a mixture of policies targeted to the particular country context. Areas for further research include a closer examination of the relationship between employment protection legislation and passive and active labor market policies. Information on the cost effectiveness of passive and active labor market policies is also thin on the ground.

Notes

1. Sanchez-Puerta (2010) cites Blunch, Canagarajah, and Raju (2001); Jutting, Xenogiani, and Parlevliet (2007); and Chen (2007).

2. Data are from Charmes (2000). The informal sector is defined as "a group of production units which form a part, within the System of National Accounts (SNA), of the household sector as unincorporated enterprises owned by households" (Sanchez-Puerta 2010, 24).

3. "The vulnerable employment indicator has some limitations: (1) wage and salary employment is not synonymous with decent work, as workers may carry a high economic risk despite the fact that they are in wage employment; (2) the unemployed are not included in the indicator, though they are vulnerable; (3) a worker may be classified in one of the two vulnerable status groups but still not carry a high economic risk, especially in the developed economies" (ILO 2011, 22).

4. Sanchez-Puerta (2010, 4) cites three examples of job security measures—ordinal indices based on statutory rules (used in OECD countries); cardinal index based on compliance costs by employer of EPL; and judgment of executives on difficulties of adjusting employment levels to economic realities.

5. Sanchez-Puerta (2010, 8) cites Betcherman, Luinstra, and Ogawa (2001); Maloney (2001); IDB (2004); World Bank (2006); Haltiwanger, Scarpetta, and Schweiger (2006); and Ahsan and Pagés (2007).

6. Sanchez-Puerta (2010, 8) cites Micevska (2004), Freeman (2007), and Heckman and Pagés (2004).

7. Sanchez-Puerta (2010, 8) cites Micco and Pagés (2006) and Haltiwanger, Scarpetta, and Vodopivec (2003) for Central and Eastern Europe, Russia, and Ukraine; Heckman and Pagés (2004) for Latin America and the Caribbean; Autor, Donohue, and Schwab (2006) for the United States; Besley and Burgess (2004) and Ahsan and Pagés (2007) for India.

8. Sanchez-Puerta (2010, 8) cites Addison and Teixeira (2001); Betcherman, Luinstra, and Ogawa (2001); World Bank (2006); and Djankov and Ramalho (2009) for Europe and Central Asian countries.

9. Sanchez-Puerta (2010, 8) cites Betcherman, Luinstra, and Ogawa (2001); Micevska (2004); Freeman (2007); and Heckman and Pages (2004).

10. Sanchez-Puerta (2010, 9) cites Besley and Burgess (2004) for India; Micco and Pages (2006) for 11 developed and 7 Latin American countries; Hoek (2007) for Brazil; and Autor, Kerr, and Kugler (2007) for the United States.

11. Sanchez-Puerta (2010, 9) cites Besley and Burgess (2004) as an exception. As shown in table 3.5, they find a positive association between urban poverty and EPL in India.

12. Approximately 20 percent of workers in Peru were entitled to severance pay in 2000 (MacIsaac and Rama 2000).

13. Vodopivec and Raju (2004) cite Subbarao (2003) for the redistributive role of public works programs in Chile and India: Haddad and Adato (2001) for programs in South Africa; and Vroman (2002) for 13 OECD countries.

14. Sanchez-Puerta (2010) cites Blanchard and Tirole (2007, 17) as being among the first to model the optimal design of employment protection and unemployment insurance together: "Optimality requires both unemployment insurance and employment protection in the form of layoff taxes."

References

Addison, J., and Paulino Teixeira. 2001. "The Economics of Employment Protection." IZA Discussion Paper 381, Institute for the Study of Labor, Bonn, Germany.

Ahsan, A., and Carmen Pagés. 2007. "Helping or Hurting Workers? Assessing the Effects of de Jure and de Facto Labor Regulation in India." Social Protection Discussion Paper 713, World Bank, Washington, DC.

Atkinson, A. B. 1995. "On Targeting Social Security: Theory and Western Experience with Family Benefits." In *Public Spending and the Poor: Theory and Evidence*, ed. D. van de Walle and K. Nead, 25–68. Baltimore: Johns Hopkins University Press.

Autor, D., J. Donohue, and Stewart Schwab. 2006. "The Costs of Wrongful-Discharge Laws." *Review of Economics and Statistics* 88 (2): 211–31.

Autor, D., W. Kerr, and Adriana D. Kugler. 2007. "Does Employment Protection Reduce Productivity? Evidence from the United States." *Economic Journal* 117 (5210): 189–217.

Barrera, F., and L. Higuera. 2004. "Characterization of Training in Colombia: Household and Firms Surveys." Background paper, World Bank, Washington, DC.

Besley, T., and Robin Burgess. 2004. "Can Labor Regulation Hinder Economic Performance? Evidence from India." *Quarterly Journal of Economics* 119 (1): 91–134.

Betcherman, G. 2002. "An Overview of Labor Market Worldwide: Key Trends and Major Policy Issues." Social Protection Discussion Paper 205, World Bank, Washington, DC.

Betcherman, G., A. Luinstra, and Makoto Ogawa. 2001. "Labor Market Regulation: International Experience in Promoting Employment and Social Protection." Social Protection Discussion Paper 128, World Bank, Washington, DC.

Betcherman, G., K. Olivas, and Amit Dar. 2004. "Impact of Active Labor Market Programs: New Evidence from Evaluations with Particular Attention to Developing and Transition Countries." Social Protection Discussion Paper 402, World Bank, Washington, DC.

Blanchard, O., and Jean Tirole. 2007. "The Joint Design of Unemployment Insurance and Employment Protection: A First Pass." CEPR Discussion Paper 6127, Center for Economic and Policy Research, Washington, DC.

Blunch, N., S. Canagarajah, and Dhushyanth Raju. 2001. "The Informal Sector Revisited: A Synthesis across Space and Time." Social Protection Discussion Paper 119, World Bank, Washington, DC.

Charmes, J. 2000. "The Contribution of Informal Sector to GDP in Developing Countries: Assessment, Estimates, Methods, Orientations for the Future."

Paper presented at meeting of the Expert Group on Informal Sector Statistics (Delhi Group), Geneva, August 28–30.

Chen, Martha. 2007. "Rethinking the Informal Economy: Linkages with the Formal Economy and the Formal Regulatory Environment." DESA Working Paper 46, Department of Economic and Social Affairs (DESA), United Nations, New York.

Chong, A., and J. Galdo. 2006. "Training and Informality in Peru." World Bank, Washington, DC.

Coady, David. 2002. "Social Safety Nets, Human Capital and the Poor: Evidence from Recent Program Evaluations." Paper prepared for the Asian Development Bank and Inter-American Development Bank workshop, "Social Protection for the Poor in Asia and Latin America: Concepts and Experiences," Manila, October 21–25.

Djankov, S., and R. Ramalho. 2009. "Employment Laws in Developing Countries." *Journal of Comparative Economics* 37: 3–13.

Freeman, R. 2007. "Labor Market Institutions around the World." Working Paper 13242, National Bureau of Economic Research, Cambridge, MA.

Friedlander, Daniel, David Greenberg, and Philip K. Robins. 1997. "Evaluating Government Training Programs for the Economically Disadvantaged." *Journal of Economic Literature* 35 (4): 1809–1955.

Haddad, L., and M. Adato. 2001. "How Efficiently Do Public Works Programs Transfer Benefits to the Poor? Evidence from South Africa." FCND DP 108. International Food Policy Research Institute, Washington, DC.

Haltiwanger, J., S. Scarpetta, and Helena Schweiger. 2006. "Assessing Job Flows across Countries: The Role of Industry, Firm Size, and Regulations." IZA Working Paper Series 4070, Institute for the Study of Labor, Bonn.

Haltiwanger, J., S. Scarpetta, and M. Vodopivec. 2003. "How Institutions Affect Labor Market Outcomes: Evidence from Transition Countries." World Bank Economists' Forum, April 10, Washington, DC.

Heckman, J., and Carmen Pagés. 2004. Introd. to *Law and Employment: Lessons from Latin America and the Caribbean*, ed. J. Heckman and Carmen Pagés. Chicago: University of Chicago Press.

Henley, A., R. Arabsheibani, and Francisco Carneiro. 2006. "On Defining and Measuring the Informal Sector." Policy Research Working Paper 3866, World Bank, Washington, DC.

Hoek, Jasper. 2007. "Labor Flows in Formal and Informal Labor Markets in Brazil." Paper presented at IZA (Institute for the Study of Labor)–World Bank Conference, "Employment and Development," June 8–9, Bonn.

Ibarraran, P., and David Rosas. 2006. "IDB's Job Training Operations: Thematic Report of Impact Evaluations." Inter-American Development Bank, Washington, DC.

Inter-American Development Bank (IDB). 2004. *Good Jobs Wanted: Labor Markets in Latin America.* Baltimore: Johns Hopkins University Press.

International Labour Organization (ILO). 2011. *Global Employment Trends.* Geneva: International Labour Organization.

Jutting, J., T. Xenogiani, and Jante Parlevliet. 2007. "Work and Well-Being: Informal Employment Revisited." Paper presented at IZA–World Bank Conference, "Employment and Development," June 8–9, Bonn.

Lazear, E. P. 1990. "Job Security Provisions and Employment." *Quarterly Journal of Economics* 105 (3): 699–726.

MacIsaac, D., and M. Rama. 2000. "Mandatory Severance Pay in Peru: An Assessment of Its Coverage and Effects Using Panel Data." Development Research Group, Public Service Delivery, World Bank, Washington, DC.

Maloney, W. 2001. "Self-Employment and Labor Turnover: Cross-Country Evidence." Proceedings, World Bank Economists Forum, Washington, DC.

Marquez, G. 2002. "Training the Workforce in Latin America: What Needs to Be Done?" IADB Labor Markets Policy Briefs Series, Inter-American Development Bank, Washington, DC.

Micco, A., and Carmen Pagés. 2006. "The Economic Effects of Employment Protection: Evidence from International Industry-Level Data." IZA Discussion Paper 2433, Institute for the Study of Labor, Bonn.

Micevska, M. 2004. "Unemployment and Labor Market Rigidities in Southeast Europe." Working paper, GDN-SEE and Vienna Institute for International Economic Studies (wiiw), Vienna.

Pagés, C., G. Pierre, and S. Scarpetta. 2009. "Job Creation in Latin America and the Caribbean: Recent Trends and the Policy Challenges." World Bank, Washington, DC.

Petrin A., and Jagadeesh Sivadasan. 2006. "Job Security Does Affect Economic Efficiency: Theory, A New Statistic, and Evidence from Chile." NBER Working Paper 12757. National Bureau of Economic Research, Cambridge, MA.

Puerto, Olga. 2007. "Interventions to Support Young Workers in Latin America and the Caribbean: Regional Report for the Youth Employment Inventory." World Bank, Washington, DC.

Ravallion, M. 1991. "Reaching the Rural Poor through Public Employment: Arguments, Evidence, and Lessons from South Asia." *World Bank Research Observer* 6 (2): 153–75.

———. 1999. "Appraising Workfare." *World Bank Research Observer* 14 (February): 31–48.

Sanchez-Puerta, M. L. 2010. "Labor Market Policy Research for Developing Countries: Recent Examples from the Literature. What Do We Know and What Should We Know?" Social Protection Discussion Paper 1001, World Bank, Washington, DC.

Spevacek, A. 2009. "Effectiveness of Active Labor Market Programs: A Review of Programs in Central and Eastern Europe and the Commonwealth of Independent States." USAID Knowledge Services Center, December 23, http://pdf.usaid.gov/pdf_docs/PNADM044.pdf.

Stanley, M., L. Katz, and A. Krueger. 1998. "Developing Skills: What We Know about the Impacts of American Employment and Training Programs on Employment, Earnings and Educational Outcomes." MalcolmWeiner Center for Social Policy Working Paper H-98-02, John F. Kennedy School of Government, Harvard University, Cambridge, MA.

Subbarao, K. 2003. "Systemic Shocks and Social Protection: Role and Effectiveness of Public Works Programs." Social Protection Discussion Paper 0302, World Bank, Washington, DC.

Tan, H., and Gladys Lopez Azevedo. 2003. "Mexico: In-Firm Training for the Knowledge Economy." Policy Research Working Paper 2957, World Bank, Washington, DC.

Vodopivec, M., and D. Raju. 2002. "Income Support Systems for the Unemployed: Issues and Options." Social Protection Discussion Paper Series 214. World Bank, Washington, DC.

———. 2004. "Income Support Systems for the Unemployed: Issues and Options." World Bank, Washington, DC.

Vroman, W. 2002. "Unemployment Insurance and Unemployment Assistance: A Comparison." Social Protection Discussion Paper 0203, Urban Institute and World Bank, Washington, DC.

World Bank. 2004. "Pending Issues in Protection, Productivity Growth, and Poverty Reduction." Executive summary of *Labor Stocktaking in the LAC Region*. World Bank, Washington, DC, http://siteresources.worldbank.org/INTLM/Resources/390041-1103750362599/LAC_paper.pdf.

———. 2006. *Enhancing Job Opportunities: Eastern Europe and the Former Soviet Union*. World Bank, Washington, DC.

———. 2008. "MILES to Go: A Quest for an Operational Labor Market Paradigm for Developing Countries. Social Protection and Labor Sector." Washington, DC: World Bank, http://siteresources.worldbank.org/INTLM/Resources/390041-1212776476091/5078455-1267646113835/MILESThequestoperationalLMparadigm_Jan212008.pdf.

CHAPTER 4

Education, Skills, and the Labor Market

This chapter examines the links between education and the labor market in developing economies. In the labor market, individuals put education to use and engage in lifelong learning. The structure of the labor market has implications for the quantity and quality of education created in an economy and for the uses to which it is put. The structure of the labor market will determine how much skilled labor goes into growth-enhancing activities. Education is also critical for technological adaptation and innovation—the drivers of economic growth.

Figure 4.1, adapted from Fasih (2008), is helpful in understanding the relationship among education, skills, and labor outcomes. A number of policies and programs have to be in place to achieve good labor outcomes. Education is a necessary condition but not sufficient, because education has to be supported by good labor market opportunities for the skilled, including macroeconomic stability, an attractive investment climate, and efficient labor markets, as well as adequate systems of social protection, among other factors.

What is known about the education-jobs nexus, and how can education improve labor market outcomes? Fasih (2008) underscores a number of interesting facts. First, literacy, numeracy, and basic cognitive skills improve individuals' economic outcomes. But it takes 8–12 years of schooling in

Figure 4.1   The Relationship among Education, Skills, and Labor Outcomes

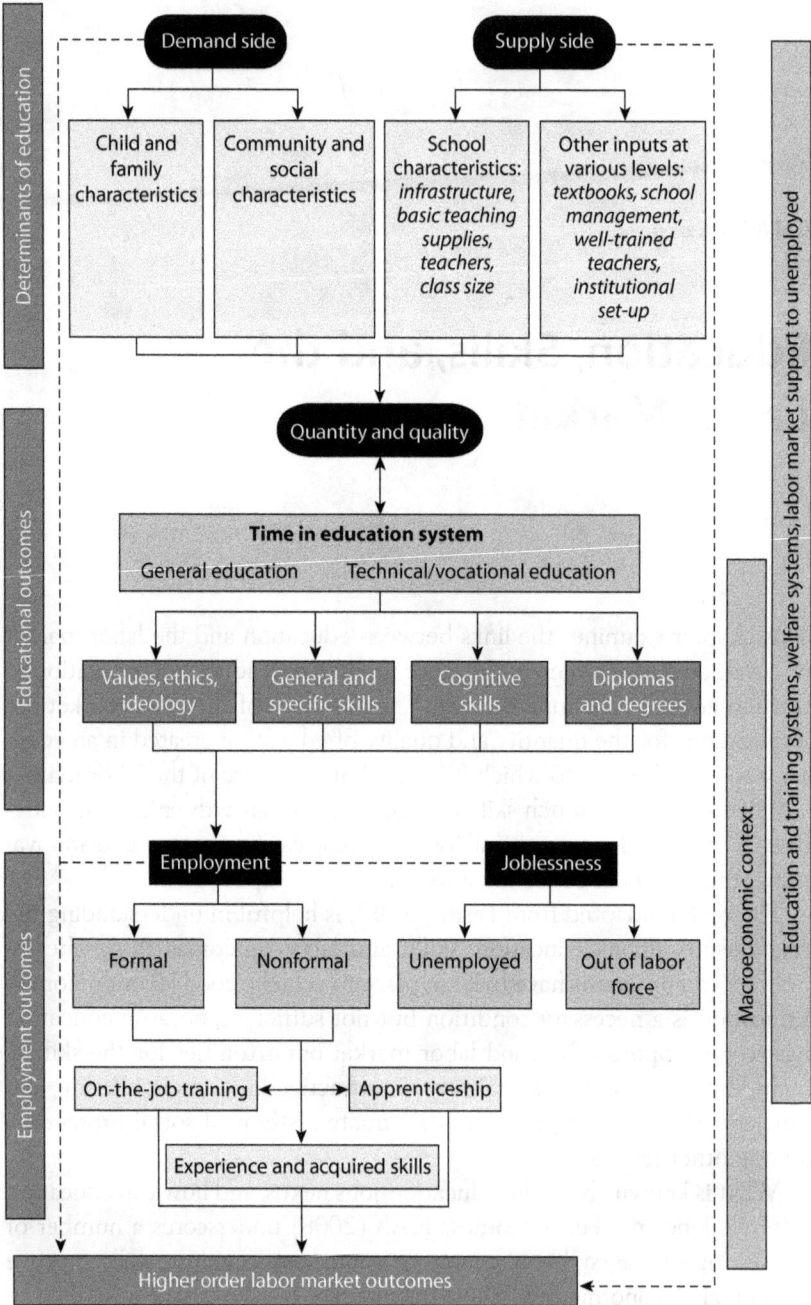

Source: Fasih 2008.

developing countries for students to become functionally literate and numerate, a finding indicative of the need to improve the quality of learning in primary educational systems.

Second, countries at different levels of economic development have diverse demands for education and skills that may or may not match the supply. For example, de Ferranti et al. (2003) suggest that whereas East Asian countries might benefit from more secondary school graduates to fill their skill gap, Latin American countries, because of their wealth of natural resources, would benefit from more experts in manufacturing processes and more tertiary education graduates.

Third, investments in early childhood development are fundamental to developing the cognitive skills of children, as these affect longer-term learning, skills development, and labor market outcomes. In the developing world, for example, many countries have introduced conditional cash transfers for families, provided that their young children are vaccinated, given regular health visits, and supplied with proper nutrition. Such programs not only help reduce the vulnerability of disadvantaged children but also tend to enhance the efficiency of early learning.

Fourth, according to a recent finding, the shape of the educational earnings profile appears to be changing from concave, in which primary education earns the highest returns, to convex, in which secondary and tertiary education earns the highest returns in the labor market. This changing profile has profound implications for the poverty-reducing effects of education. For instance, the Millennium Development Goals (MDGs) assume that the completion of basic education, along with the attainment of other MDGs, will help realize the goal of halving world poverty by 2015. If, however, the relationship of education and earnings is convex (or even linear), then expanding enrollment only at lower levels of education will not raise earnings substantially and consequently will not prove to be an effective means of helping people out of poverty.

Fifth, rapid globalization is dramatically increasing global demand for skills and the development of skills-biased technology and innovation. As a result, the returns to primary education may indeed be low. In addition, those returns, especially in developing nations, could be low because the educational systems are failing to produce minimum functional literacy and numeracy skills at the primary level. In either case, the provision of high-quality subsidized primary education is warranted, not only because it empowers people and helps reduce inequality but also because countries with low levels of education are at risk of remaining trapped in technological stagnation and low growth (de Ferranti et al. 2003).

Sixth, research also suggests that not all individuals benefit from education equally, meaning that labor market outcomes are heterogeneous. Analysis of the returns to education across a conditional earnings distribution shows increasing, decreasing, or constant returns by quantiles, depending on the country. For the limited number of countries for which evidence exists, returns to education appear to increase by quintile in more-developed countries and to decrease in developing countries. The increasing returns to education from the lower to the higher end of the earnings distribution indicate that ability and education complement each other. The relationship depends on the country context; the policy implications for heterogeneity must be interpreted in light of the broader context of a given labor market.

Seventh, in a perfectly competitive labor market, noncognitive skills such as self-confidence, self-motivation, and ability may have higher value, and thus people with higher ability may reap higher returns. Certain types of mentoring programs, such as the Big Brother or Big Sister programs in the United States, may also help develop such noncognitive skills. In countries with large disparities in the quality of education between the rich and the poor—and where individuals are systematically sorted into high-quality schools by wealth—the poor will attain fewer skills for the same "quantity" of education. The policy option in such a case would be to counter the sorting process through the provision of choice of better schooling through, for example, school vouchers or better-quality publicly funded private schools for the poor (Angrist, Bettinger, and Kremer 2006; Barrera-Osorio 2007).

Overall, schooling can substitute for and reinforce ability, and, in that sense, education can play an equity-enhancing or inequality-reducing role. A holistic analysis of education and labor demand, one that analyzes education in a broader macroeconomic context, helps ensure a correct diagnostic response. The demand for new and more skills is not always met. In fact, the world is witnessing a huge mismatch between the supply of and demand for skills (see figure 4.2). In 2010, for example, Manpower Inc. surveyed 35,000 employers in 36 countries and territories to determine the impact of this shortage on the local labor market. The survey found that 31 percent of employers worldwide are having difficulty filling positions due to a lack of suitable available talent. The top five jobs that employers have most difficulty in filling are, ranked in order: skilled trades, sales representatives, technicians, engineers, and accounting and finance staff (Manpower 2010a).

It is interesting to note that excess demand for skilled workers and excess supply of low-skilled workers coexist in almost all countries.

Figure 4.2   Disconnect between Demand for and Supply of Skills

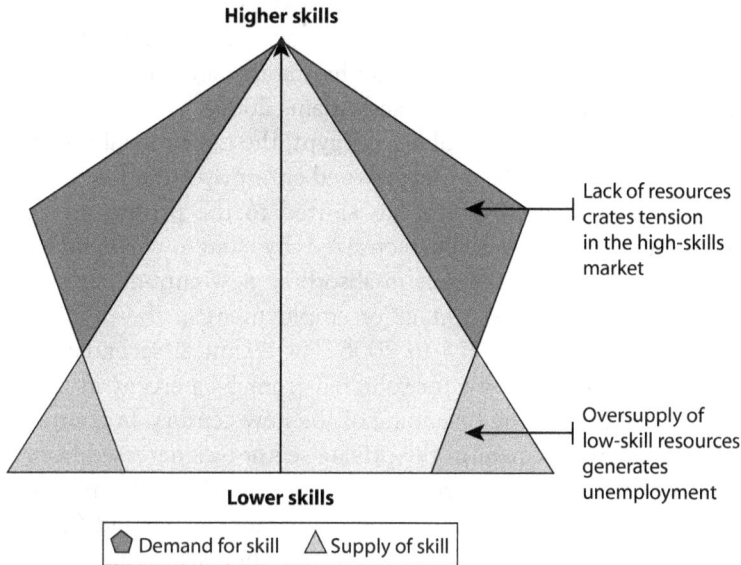

Source: Manpower 2010b, 3.

According to the U.S. Bureau of Labor Statistics, in August 2010 the unemployment rate in the United States was 9.5 percent, with 15 million people looking for jobs. However, according to Manpower Inc. (2010a), 3 million jobs remained unfilled in the country.

The oversupply of certain types of workers indicates an educational system that lacks relevance and quality and thus is failing to respond to the changing demand for skills in labor markets. In the case of the eastern Caribbean states, where the service sector is an important part of the economy, about three-fourths of new jobs in 2006 were in tourism. However, firms have difficulties in finding employees such as chefs and managers that possess specific skills in this sector, a shortage that results in the hiring of foreign experts (World Bank 2007b). In the Philippines, companies in the manufacturing and service sectors encounter problems in finding workers with the appropriate skills to fill positions as directors and managers, as well as openings for professional and administrative positions (di Gropello 2010).

Many educational systems are still operating under the influence of old traditions or colonial influence, in isolation from real market conditions. For example, curricula in Mozambique developed 20 years ago overemphasize the needs of a centrally planned economy and employment in large state-owned enterprises. TVET[1] in most French-speaking African countries, moreover, follows the French model of the 1960s, which features excessive school-based curricula and lacks the flexibility to respond to market needs. While such a model has disappeared in France itself, it is still visible in Africa (Johanson and Adams 2004).

Similarly in the Arab Republic of Egypt, the educational system still prepares students for jobs in state-owned enterprises and bureaucracies, while the demand for workers has shifted to the private sector. The public sector in Egypt is characterized by state-owned enterprises, which used to play a major role in absorbing new entrants into the job market. However, the percentage of employment in the public sector decreased sharply from 1975 to 2006. For technical secondary graduates, the share of public sector jobs fell from 54 percent in the mid-1970s to 5 percent at the beginning of the new century. In contrast, the proportion of employment in the private sector has increased from one-half to two-thirds of these graduates, with informal private employment representing 56 percent of all employment among males and 42 percent among females (Amer 2007). Skills requirements for the formal and informal sectors differ in that the informal sector requires entrepreneurship and multiple skills. This mismatch in supply and demand translates into limited opportunities for young people to participate fully in the economy.

India and China currently represent 40 percent of the world's supply of labor. However, the labor market is sending a strong message that educational systems based on rote memorization do not develop soft skills and are not delivering relevant, marketable skills. For example, multinational corporations consider only 1 in 10 of China's 600,000 engineers that graduate each year employable (McGregor 2006). Similarly, out of 3 million students who graduate from Indian universities every year, only 25 percent of engineering graduates and 10–15 percent of general college graduates are considered suitable for direct employment in the offshore information technology and business process outsourcing industries.

Moving Forward to Improve Educational Flexibility, Skills, and Employability

Priorities and strategies for making educational systems flexible, providing relevant skills, and improving employability vary, depending on a country's developmental level, speed of economic growth, and state of secondary education. Economic growth was selected as a factor because growth generates demand and demand determines the scale of skills and TVET. In addition, secondary education is fundamental to skills development. For example, fast-growing economies require a more skilled workforce to support rapid growth than do slow-growing economies; expanding TVET thus becomes a priority.

For rapidly growing economies in low-income countries that have low secondary education enrollment, the priority is to develop secondary education and secondary-level TVET. For rapidly growing economies in middle-income countries, the priority is to develop tertiary TVET, as secondary education enrollment rates are generally high in those countries. Low-income countries, in general, have lower enrollment in secondary education than do middle-income countries, but there are exceptions. Within Africa, for example, Kenya has a much higher enrollment rate in secondary education than do other African countries. In many East Asian countries, enrollment at this level is much higher than in Africa and South Asia. Therefore, the task for certain East Asian countries will be to strengthen the quality of secondary education and develop two-year and short-term training at the tertiary level.

Countries can be grouped into four categories to identify the issues and strategies relevant to each: low- and middle-income countries with economies that are either rapidly or slowly growing (see figure 4.3; country categories correspond to the quadrants of the figure). The gross secondary education enrollment rate is used as an indicator of a country's income and growth levels.

The framework shown in figure 4.3 is intended to provide general recommendations for improving educational systems in the three areas discussed in the previous section: developing a flexible educational system, building relevant skills and competencies, and strengthening school-to-work links.

Whether a country is low or middle income, and whether it has a rapidly or a slowly growing economy, a holistic policy and strategy should be pursued to reach balanced, sustainable development. Countries in all four quadrants of figure 4.3 thus need to prioritize their policies and strategies based on their own economic and educational development needs. Table 4.1 below summarizes policy priorities and options for increasing the flexibility of the educational system, skills development, and employability.

Figure 4.3   Stages of Development and Educational Needs

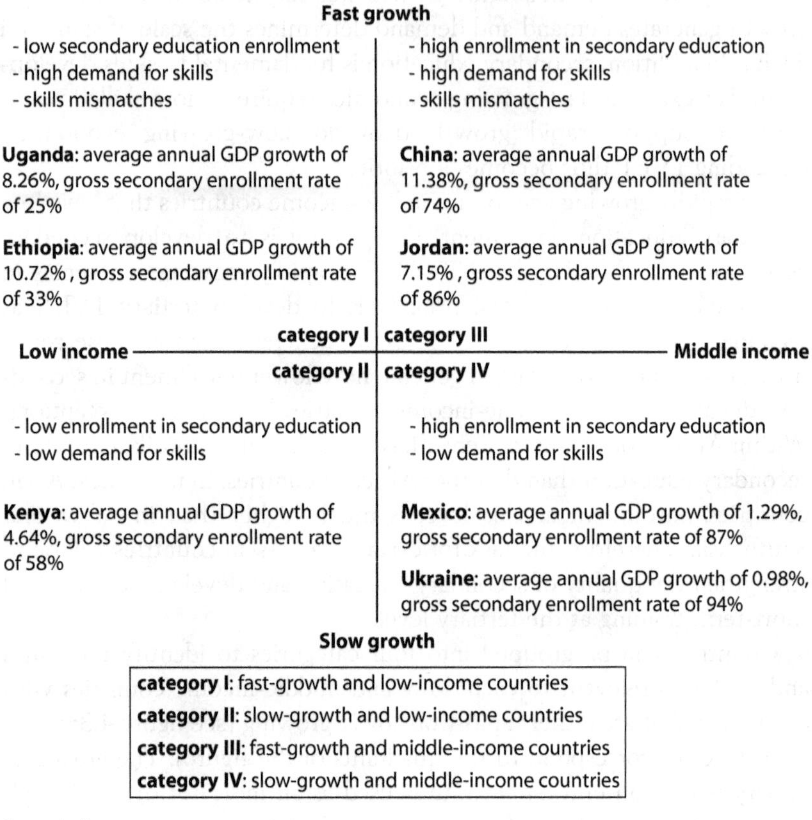

Fast growth

- low secondary education enrollment - high demand for skills - skills mismatches	- high enrollment in secondary education - high demand for skills - skills mismatches
Uganda: average annual GDP growth of 8.26%, gross secondary enrollment rate of 25%	**China**: average annual GDP growth of 11.38%, gross secondary enrollment rate of 74%
Ethiopia: average annual GDP growth of 10.72%, gross secondary enrollment rate of 33%	**Jordan**: average annual GDP growth of 7.15%, gross secondary enrollment rate of 86%

Low income ——————— category I | category III ——————— **Middle income**
                        category II | category IV

- low enrollment in secondary education - low demand for skills	- high enrollment in secondary education - low demand for skills
Kenya: average annual GDP growth of 4.64%, gross secondary enrollment rate of 58%	**Mexico**: average annual GDP growth of 1.29%, gross secondary enrollment rate of 87%
	Ukraine: average annual GDP growth of 0.98%, gross secondary enrollment rate of 94%

Slow growth

> **category I**: fast-growth and low-income countries
> **category II**: slow-growth and low-income countries
> **category III**: fast-growth and middle-income countries
> **category IV**: slow-growth and middle-income countries

Source: Authors.
Note: The classification of countries in the matrix is based on World Bank country classifications: low income, middle income, or high income, as determined by 2009 gross national income per capita. For details, see World Bank Web page on classifications, http://data.worldbank.org/about/country-classifications. Data sources for average gross domestic product (GDP) growth rates are the Global Development Finance and World Development Indicators databases of the World Bank, http://data.worldbank.org/data-catalog; the source for gross secondary education enrollment rates is World Bank 2010. Average GDP growth rates are cited for years between 2005 and 2009; gross secondary enrollment rates are based on 2008 data.

Skills in a Knowledge Economy

With sustained use and creation of knowledge at the center of the economic development process, an economy essentially becomes a knowledge economy. A knowledge economy is one that utilizes knowledge as the key engine of economic growth. It is an economy where knowledge is acquired, created, disseminated, and used effectively to enhance economic development. To better account for the various dimensions of

Table 4.1 Education Policy Priorities and Options for Developing Countries, by Category

	Category I: low income and fast growth	*Category II:* low income and slow growth	*Category III:* middle income and fast growth	*Category IV:* middle income and slow growth
Flexibility	• Expand access to secondary education • Develop TVET and short-term training programs for skills needs • Provide financial subsidies to poor students to attend TVET • Consider making secondary TVET institutions flexible with short- and long-term training	• Expand access to secondary education and prepare the talent pool for future growth • Develop TVET with a focus on entrepreneurship and self-employment training • Build smooth pathways between general education and TVET	• Provide second-chance and skills development opportunities for youth and adults • Make college the most flexible part of the system • Develop TVET and short-term training for skills needs	• Build a lifelong learning system and the talent pool for future growth • Provide second-chance learning opportunities and validate nonformal and informal learning experiences
Skills	• Partner with industries and sectors to identify future skills needs and maintain relevance of school courses and qualifications • Balance training of low, medium, and high skills • Focus on the training of new and soft skills and their assessment	• Update learning contents and train teachers to develop new and soft skills • Strengthen basic skills, identify and focus on new and soft skills	• Partner with industries and sectors to identify future skills needs and maintain relevance of school courses and qualifications • Balance training of low, medium, and high skills • Focus on the training of new and soft skills and their assessment	• Update learning contents and train teachers for new and soft skills • Strengthen training in new and soft skills
Employability	• Establish links with and incentives for industries to participate in TVET programs and provide work experience • Develop a public information system, career guidance, and employment support system	• Develop a public information system, career guidance, and employment support system	• Establish links with and incentives for industries to participate in TVET programs and provide work experience • Develop a public information system, career guidance, and employment support system	• Develop a public information system, career guidance, and employment support system

Source: Authors.

85

knowledge, the World Bank has developed the Knowledge Economy Framework.

It has been found that the successful transition to the knowledge economy typically involves elements such as long-term investments in education, developing innovation capability, modernizing the information infrastructure, and having an economic environment conducive to market transactions. The case of Tunisia is instructive (see box 4.1). These elements have been termed by the World Bank *the pillars* of the knowledge economy and together they constitute the Knowledge Economy Framework:

- An economic incentive and institutional regime that provides good economic policies and institutions that permit efficient mobilization and allocation of resources and stimulate creativity and incentives for the efficient creation, dissemination, and use of existing knowledge.
- Educated and skilled workers who can continuously upgrade and adapt their skills to efficiently create and use knowledge.
- An effective innovation system of firms, research centers, universities, consultants, and other organizations that can keep up with the knowledge revolution and tap into the growing stock of global knowledge and assimilate and adapt it to local needs.
- A modern and adequate information infrastructure that can facilitate the effective communication, dissemination, and processing of information and knowledge.

The Knowledge Economy Framework thus asserts that investments in the four pillars are necessary for sustained creation, adoption, adaptation, and use of knowledge in domestic economic production, which will consequently result in higher-value-added goods and services. These investments would tend to increase the probability of economic success, and hence economic development, in the current highly competitive and globalized world economy.

Although research on the effects of the knowledge economy on employment creation is still at a preliminary stage, efforts have begun, particularly in advanced economies, to quantify its effect. Using Eurostat data, Brinkley and Lee (2006) studied the rate of job creation in knowledge-based sectors and low-knowledge sectors in the European Union and the United States over a 10-year period. They found that knowledge-based industries created twice as many new jobs in the United States and four times as many in Europe (see table 4.2).

Table 4.2   Change in Employment in Knowledge-Based Industries in Europe and the United States, 1995–2005

(percent)

Knowledge-based	United States	European Union 15
High-medium tech manufacturing	−15.7	−2.4
Knowledge-based services	27.2	30.7
All knowledge-based industries	20.9	23.9
Low-medium tech manufacturing	−18.3	−7.5
Less knowledge-based services	12.7	13.5
All nonknowledge-based industries	10.2	5.7
Total employment	14.0	12.6

Source: Brinkley and Lee 2006.
Note: U.S. figures are based on Work Foundation estimates, using U.S. Bureau of Labor Statistics data. Percentages for the United States refer to employees; percentages for the European Union refer to total employment.

The Eurostat definition of knowledge-based industries is based on four-digit Standard Industrial Classification (SIC) codes used by the Organisation for Economic Co-operation and Development. It covers employment in, among other areas, telecommunications, software and research, and certain public sector activities including health, social work, and education. Less knowledge-based industries and services include medium- and low-tech manufacturing, construction, agriculture, energy and water, retail, hospitality, and all other services. Table 4.3 shows that employment growth in knowledge-based industries exceeded that of nonknowledge-based industries by twice as much in the United States and four times as much among the EU15 countries.[2]

At the national level, all EU15 states saw growth in knowledge-based industries exceed that in the rest of the economy. In several economies, the only net expansion in employment was in the knowledge-based industries.

For the years 1995–2005, knowledge-based services have been growing twice as fast as other services across the EU15. Of the 21 million jobs created in services in this period, nearly 14 million or two-thirds were in knowledge-based services (table 4.4).

Innovation and Employment Creation

As mentioned above, because knowledge is inherently difficult to measure, the literature on the employment effects of the knowledge economy is very thin. However, one promising strand of literature focuses on the

Table 4.3   Change in Employment in Knowledge-Based and Nonknowledge-Based Industries in Europe, 1995–2005
(percent)

Change in employment	Knowledge-based industries	All other industries
Spain	74.6	42.4
Ireland	70.7	42.9
Greece	36.8	8.3
Netherlands	29.9	12.3
Finland	29.6	13.5
Italy	28.4	4.1
EU15	23.9	5.7
Belgium	23.3	3.7
Austria	18.3	−5.4
Germany	17.1	−8.6
United Kingdom	16.7	1.0
France	16.3	7.3
Sweden	12.8	2.0
Denmark	11.6	−0.2
Portugal	11.1	1.4

Source: Brinkley and Lee 2006.
Note: Knowledge-based industries follow the Eurostat definition; other industries include medium- to low-tech manufacturing, construction, agriculture, energy and water, retail, hospitality, and all other services. Data for Portugal are for 1998–2005.

Table 4.4   Change in Employment in Knowledge-Based and Nonknowledge-Based Service Industries in Europe, 1995–2005

EU15	Change in number of jobs (thousands)	Change in number of jobs (%)
Business and communications	5,090	54.5
High-tech services	1,581	37.1
Health, education	6,838	26.7
Financial services	129	2.5
All knowledge services	13,637	30.7
Less-knowledge-intense services	6,945	13.5

Source: Brinkley and Lee 2006.
Note: Education and health include recreational and cultural; business and communications include some travel services.

employment effects of a critical aspect of the knowledge economy, innovation. As Edmund Phelps noted in a *New York Times* article: "High employment depends on a high level of investment activity…. Sustained business investment, in turn, rests on innovation…innovation creates jobs across the economy, for entrepreneurs, marketers and buyers" (August 6, 2010).

Box 4.1

Knowledge-Based Development and Employment in Tunisia

Until recently, Tunisia was typical of an economy that had developed a strong industrial base in sectors such as textiles (50 percent of manufacturing employment) and electronics by attracting foreign investors. The success of these industries owed much to a pragmatic policy comprising significant improvements to the business environment, strong tax incentives, and investment in labor force qualifications. These industries, however—and therefore the economy—have been experiencing a certain loss of competitiveness. Moreover, despite a relatively high growth rate—5 percent over the past 10 years—Tunisia is facing huge unemployment rates, notably among university graduates: 50,000 arrive in the job market each year, and more than 70 percent do not find a job.

To counter these trends, the Tunisian government had in the previous decade made progress on the education and information and communications technology (ICT) pillars. University enrollment increased from 23 percent in 2001 to 32 percent in 2004, while enrollment in short-term technical programs was up from 21 percent in 2001 to 25 percent in 2004. On the ICT front, Tunisia devoted more than 7 percent of its GDP to ICT expenses. Some 30,000 jobs were created in the sector during the second half of the previous decade. Telephone penetration is increasing rapidly, thanks to mobile phones, but computer and Internet penetration is still low, with less than 10 percent of the population using the Internet. Measures to improve the innovation system include an increase in public research and development expenses, doubling in five years to reach some 0.8 percent of GDP; the implementation of a large-scale program, largely financed by the European Union, to upgrade the technical and organizational capabilities of established enterprises (more than 2,300 enterprises have benefited from the program in 10 years); and the planning of 10 "technopoles," of which the most advanced is El Gazala, in place since 2000, in the telecommunications sector. For employment, results are not negligible, although many jobs are related to the public sector.

Source: World Bank 2007a.

Theoretical contributions analyzing the effect of innovation on employment at the firm level stress the importance of a distinction between product and process innovations. For neither type of innovation, however, is the overall effect on a firm's demand for labor clear.

Product innovations that lead to new products on the market tend to stimulate a new demand. This new demand would allow innovating firms to hire more workers. Thus, one would expect product innovations to have a direct positive effect on employment. But there could also be a less obvious secondary indirect effect: if a firm introduces a new product to the market and there are no direct competitors yet, the innovating firm could benefit from a temporary monopoly position until other firms introduce similar or better products. In this short-run market position, the firm can exploit its monopoly power and maximize its profits. The firm could then reduce its output and its employment. This effect runs opposite to the direct effect. Thus, the overall effect of product innovations on employment is unclear in theory.

For process innovations the direct effect is also obvious. A process innovation is an improvement in the production process, which aims at improving the productivity of inputs, such as labor. Thus, the firm is able to produce the same level of output with fewer workers. From this standpoint, one would expect process innovations to have a direct negative effect on employment. But a secondary indirect effect must also be considered in this case. The firm can produce its output at lower costs after the implementation of the process innovation. If the firm passes on this cost advantage to the price of the output good, the quantity demanded for this good should increase and the resulting increased output would allow the firm to hire additional workers. Because this effect might outweigh the productivity effect, it is therefore again not possible to draw a definite theoretical conclusion about the direction of the effect of process innovations on labor demand (Lachenmaier and Rottman 2007).

The most direct employment impact of innovation is found in the firms that introduce them. The evidence available suggests that firms innovating in products, but also in processes, grow faster and are more likely to expand their employment than noninnovative ones, regardless of industry, size, or other characteristics.

Based on the British industrial relations survey on the adoption of information and communication technology (ICT) in the workplace and a variety of measures of innovation, studies by Machin and Wadhwani (1991); Blanchflower, Millward, and Oswald (1991); and Blanchflower and Burgess (1998) have found that innovation has had a positive impact on jobs. Blanchflower and Burgess (1998) also found similar but weaker evidence for Australia. For German firms, Entorf and Pohlmeir (1990) have related innovation, export, and employment in a cross-section of firms, finding a positive effect for product innovation and no effect for process innovations.

Brouwer, Kleinknecht, and Reijnen. (1993) use two innovation surveys for the Netherlands to estimate the effects of innovation on employment growth rates. They find a negative effect for overall research and development (R&D) investments but a positive effect for product-related R&D. In Norway, Klette and Forre (1998) have found a negative association between R&D and employment at the plant level. Moreover, new technologies are often linked to innovations in organizations; Greenan (2003) has considered a large and representative sample of French firms that introduced advanced manufacturing systems in 1988–93, finding that firms innovating in both technologies and organizations have created more jobs than firms introducing only the latter and than noninnovators.

However, firm-level studies cannot identify whether the gains of innovating firms are made at the expense of competitors or whether there is a net effect on aggregate industry. Greenan and Guellec (2000) use a 1991 French innovation survey to analyze employment growth during the period 1986–90. They find positive effects for both process and product innovation at the firm level, with the effect of product innovation being higher. However, at the industry level only product innovation was associated with employment creation; the positive effects of process innovation disappeared at the industry level.

Industry-level studies are therefore particularly important because they can identify the overall effect of technological change within a sector and account for both the direct impact on innovating firms and the indirect externalities that affect the industry as a whole. According to studies on industries, the sources and opportunities for technological change and job creation are specific to individual manufacturing and service industries, and such factors are key determinants of employment performance.

In summary, innovation appears to have a net job-creating effect in those manufacturing and service industries with high growth in demand and an orientation toward product innovation, while new processes result in job losses. The overall effect of innovative efforts depends on the countries and periods considered, but in general the effect is more positive the higher the demand growth, the greater the importance of highly innovative industries (both in manufacturing and services), and the stronger the orientation toward product innovation. A major lesson for research and policy on innovation and employment creation is that a clear distinction is needed between product innovation (with job-creating effects) and process innovation (usually with negative employment effects).

Notes

1. TVET is defined as "those aspects of educational process involving—in addition to general education—the study of technologies and related sciences and the acquisition of practical skills, attitudes, understanding and knowledge relating to occupations in various sectors of economic life" (UNESCO 2010, 5).

2. EU15 area countries are Austria, Belgium, Denmark, Finland, France, Germany, Greece, Ireland, Italy, Luxembourg, the Netherlands, Portugal, Spain, Sweden, and the United Kingdom.

References

Amer, M. 2007. *Transition from Education to Work: Egypt Country Report.* Turin: European Training Foundation.

Angrist J., E. Bettinger, and M. Kremer. 2006. "Long-Term Educational Consequences of Secondary School Vouchers: Evidence from Administrative Records in Colombia." *American Economic Review* 96 (3): 847–62.

Barrera-Osorio, F. 2007. "The Impact of Private Provision of Public Education: Empirical Evidence from Bogota's Concession Schools." Policy Research Working Paper 4121, World Bank, Washington, DC.

Blanchflower, D., and S. Burgess. 1998. "New Technology and Jobs: Comparative Evidence from a Two Country Study." *Economics of Innovation and New Technology* 5 (nos. 2/4): 109.

Blanchflower, D., N. Millward, and A. Oswald. 1991. "Unionisation and Employment Behaviour." *Economic Journal* 101(407): 815–34.

Brinkley, Ian, and Neil Lee. 2006. *The Knowledge Economy in Europe: A Report Prepared for the 2007 EU Spring Council.* London: Work Foundation.

Brouwer, E., A. Kleinknecht, and J. Reijnen. 1993. "Employment Growth and Innovation at the Firm Level: An Empirical Study." *Journal of Evolutionary Economics* 3 (2): 153–59.

De Ferranti, David, William F. Maloney, Guillermo E. Perry, Indermit Gill, J. Luis Guasch, Carolina Sanchez-Paramo, and Norbert Schady. 2003. *Closing the Gap in Education and Technology.* Latin American and Caribbean Studies Series. Washington, DC: World Bank.

Di Gropello, E., with H. Tan and P. Tandon. 2010. *Skills for the Labor Market in the Philippines.* Washington, DC: World Bank.

Entorf, H., and W. Pohlmeir. 1990. "Employment, Innovation and Export Activity." In *Microeconometrics: Surveys and Applications*, ed. J. Florens et al. Oxford: Basil Blackwell.

Fasih, Tazneen. 2008. "Linking Education Policy to Labor Market Outcomes." Discussion paper, World Bank, Washington, DC.

Greenan, N. 2003. "Organisational Change, Technology, Employment and Skills: An Empirical Study of French Manufacturing." *Cambridge Journal of Economics* 27 (2): 287–316.

Greenan, N., and D. Guellec. 2000. "Technological Innovation and Employment Reallocation." *Labour* 14 (4): 547–90.

Johanson, R. K., and A. V. Adams. 2004. *Skills Development in Sub-Saharan Africa.* World Bank Regional and Sectoral Studies. Washington, DC: World Bank.

Klette, T., and S. Førre. 1998. "Innovation and Job Creation in a Small Open Economy: Evidence from Norwegian Manufacturing Plants 1982–92." *Economics of Innovation and New Technology* 5 (nos. 2/4): 247–72.

Lachenmaier Stefan, and Horst Rottmann. 2007. "Effects of Innovation on Employment: A Dynamic Panel Analysis." Working Paper 2015, CESifo Group (Center for Economic Studies, the Ifo Institute for Economic Research, and the CESifo Munich Society for the Promotion of Economic Research), Munich.

Machin, S., and S. Wadhwani. 1991. "The Effects of Unions on Organisational Change and Employment: Evidence from WIRS." *Economic Journal* 101 (407): 324–30.

Manpower, Inc. 2010a. *Talent Shortage Survey Results.* New York: Manpower Inc., http://us.manpower.com/us/en/multimedia/Global-Shortage-Survey-Results. pdf.

———. 2010b. *Fresh Perspectives: Teachable Fit: A New Approach for Easing the Talent Mismatch.* New York: Manpower Inc., http://www.schwabfound.org/ partners_logos/pdf/3173/21334.pdf.

McGregor, R. 2006. "Up to the Job? How India and China Risk Being Stifled by a Skills Squeeze." *Financial Times,* July 20, http://www.ft.com/intl/cms/ s/0/82beabec-1787-11db-abad-0000779e2340.html#axzz1TV7YtRC8.

Phelps, Edmund S. 2010. Op-ed. "The Economy Needs a Bit of Ingenuity." *New York Times.* August 6.

UNESCO (United Nations Educational, Scientific, and Cultural Organization). 2010. *Guidelines for TVET Policy Review.* New York: United Nations, http:// unesdoc.unesco.org/images/0018/001874/187487e.pdf.

World Bank. 2007a. *Building Knowledge Economies: Advanced Strategies for Development* Washington, DC: World Bank.

———. 2007b. *Haiti Education for All Adaptable Program Grant. Report 38600* Human Development Sector, Latin America and Caribbean Region. Washington, DC: World Bank.

———. 2010. *World Development Indicators.* Washington, DC: World Bank.

CHAPTER 5

Entrepreneurship, Growth, and Job Creation

This chapter discusses entrepreneurship along three key dimensions: development and growth, job creation, and female entrepreneurship. Entrepreneurship—the process of identifying opportunities, allocating resources, and creating value—has long been described as an engine of economic growth. The entrepreneur in the Schumpeterian sense is one who through the act of "creative destruction"[1] transforms industries. The same principle of creative destruction can be applied to economies. The entrepreneur brings about, through the process of entrepreneurship, the structural transformation that facilitates the move from a traditional agrarian base to an industrial base to a service-led economy.

Notwithstanding this transformative role, the entrepreneur has been more or less absent from the economic development literature. In recent years, however, the fields of entrepreneurship and development have converged.[2] One of the key drivers of this convergence has been the focus on institutions[3] by the academic and development community and the greater role being ascribed to the private sector in development programs.

Creating jobs in the private sector depends on high-expectation and high-growth entrepreneurship. Often entrepreneurs do not carry the aspirations of high expectation and high growth for their enterprises. The reasons depend on the type of entrepreneurship, the cultural and social context, and income.

The welfare-enhancing role of women in development is strengthened further by female entrepreneurship. The number of women in entrepreneurship is lower than that of men across income groups and within and between regions. As a research topic, gender differences in entrepreneurship and the causes of these differences are still in their infancy with some emerging inferences.

Defining and Measuring Entrepreneurship

Entrepreneurship is a process, a means by which an individual makes use of or exploits opportunities in the marketplace for profit. Kirzner (1973) identified the profit motive of the entrepreneur. As a process, entrepreneurship takes places at all stages of the firm's life cycle, from inception to exit. The goal for the economy is that these opportunities be productive and contribute to economic growth and development, fostering job creation and innovation. Unproductive entrepreneurship (Baumol 1990) or rent seeking (Krueger 1974) hinders growth and development, and an important role exists for policy and institutions to mitigate the factors that contribute to unproductive entrepreneurship. Moreover, entrepreneurial activities may take place in the informal sector, particularly in economies with weak institutional frameworks or an overly regulated business environment that does not foster entrepreneurship.

Entrepreneurship may or may not be associated with innovation. While innovation was a characteristic associated with the entrepreneur as defined by Schumpeter (1961), for example, Baumol (1990) identified the replicate role of the entrepreneur. This type of entrepreneurship imitates rather than innovates.

Entrepreneurship is embraced by many disciplines across psychology, management, and economics, and measurement is influenced by the underlying academic approach. Entrepreneurship is most often measured by the rate of self-employment, business ownership, or the rate of new start-ups, the assumption being that the motivation underlying these measures is "entrepreneurship." The Global Entrepreneurship Monitor (GEM)[4] differentiates between those individuals who are entrepreneurs by necessity and those who are entrepreneurs by choice. The most recent survey by GEM[5] surveyed 175,000 people from 59 economies representing 52 percent of the world's population and 84 percent of the world's gross domestic product (GDP).

Entrepreneurship and Development Economics

Over the past 50 years, the research on entrepreneurship and development economics evolved independently of one another, according to Naudé (2010a, 1) in "relative isolation" from each other. He cites several reasons:

- The bulk of the literature on entrepreneurship is concerned with the process of entrepreneurship—the choice to become an entrepreneur, the characteristics of the entrepreneur, and the growth, success, failure, and exit of entrepreneurs from the market.
- Development economics has ignored the entrepreneur, a fact that may be related to the following:
  - The difficulty of modeling the entrepreneur in theories of development
  - The belief that entrepreneurship is not a binding constraint on development.

In recent decades, however, the entrepreneur had made it into the development literature. More and better data on the process of entrepreneurship have facilitated the formal modeling of the entrepreneur within development economics. *Entrepreneur* has become less vague a concept, and scholarly research and journal articles have tested hypotheses and modeled the impact of entrepreneurship on growth and development and vice versa.

While the data indicate that entrepreneurship is not a binding constraint in developing economies[6]—start-up rates and self-employment data all show similar, if not higher, levels of entrepreneurship in developing economies—the incentive structure of the developing economy may constrain the potential of entrepreneurship. Such economic constraints come into play when the activities of the entrepreneur go toward unproductive means. To explain the relative economic performance of developing countries, Stiglitz (2006, 7) believed that these incentive structures resulted either in a "rent economy" or in a "productive economy." A rent economy has the following characteristics:

- Failure to grow and develop
- Failure to allow entrepreneurs to play a role in the structural transformation of the economy
- Failure to distribute incomes and resources
- Concentration of income and wealth in the hands of a few elites

- Perpetuation of product-market imperfections, in particular the development of a vibrant financial sector.

To summarize, it is not entrepreneurship per se that is lacking; rather, "entrepreneurship is a conduit through which binding institutional constraints are transmitted to economic outcomes" (Naudé 2010a, 5). Herein lies the potential, as entrepreneurs are not passive actors but seek to change the status quo and will, with the right incentives, change institutions. Naudé (2010a, 5) concludes that despite the dangers of unproductive entrepreneurship, entrepreneurship in developing economies enhances welfare, first, because entrepreneurship drives structural change and economic growth, thereby opening up further opportunities for more productive wage employment, specialization, and labor mobility; and, second, because it allows people to escape from both absolute and relative poverty and informality.

Entrepreneurship, Growth, and Structural Transformation

As noted above, the entrepreneur can play a key role in bringing about a structural transformation of the economy from an agricultural, rural base to one that is more urban and manufacturing and service based. Structural transformation of an economy also lies at the heart of development economics as the Lewis (1954) model[7] of structural change attests. Furthermore, it informs the classification of economies used by the GEM. The GEM categorizes participating economies on two levels—development based and geographic location. The development-based categories arise from the World Economic Forum's (WEF) *Global Competitiveness Report* (2004), which identifies three phases of economic development based on per capita GDP and the share of exports comprising primary goods. Based on this classification, three phases of development are identified:

- *Factor-driven economies.* Economies in which agriculture and natural resource industries dominate and that are heavily reliant on labor.
- *Efficiency-driven economies.* Economies that have transitioned, or are in the process of transitioning, to manufacturing that show an increased reliance on economies of scale, and that feature more large, capital-intensive industries.
- *Innovation-driven economies.* Economies in which firms become more knowledge intensive and the service sector is expanding (Kelley, Bosma, and Amorós 2011, 7).

The GEM classification is shown in table 5.1.

The type of entrepreneurship in an economy has implications for its growth and development. The GEM differentiates between total entrepreneurial activity (TEA), which comprises nascent entrepreneurs and business owners in operation for 3.5 years; established business owners (anything greater than 3.5 years in business); and discontinued entrepreneurs. According to the GEM, the TEA represents "dynamic firm activity— the extent new businesses are introduced to a national population" (Kelley,

Table 5.1   GEM Classification by Economy and Geography

	Factor driven	Efficiency driven	Innovation driven
Sub-Saharan Africa	Angola*, Ghana, Uganda, Zambia	South Africa	
Middle East/North Africa (MENA) - South Asia	Arab Rep. of Egypt*, Islamic Rep. of Iran*, Pakistan, Saudi Arabia*, West Bank and Gaza	Tunisia	Israel
Latin America and the Caribbean	Bolivia, Guatemala*, Jamaica*	Argentina, Brazil, Chile*, Colombia, Costa Rica, Ecuador, Mexico, Peru, Trinidad and Tobago*, Uruguay*	
Eastern Europe		Bosnia and Herzegovina, Croatia*, Hungary*, Latvia*, FYR Macedonia, Montenegro, Romania, Russian Federation, Turkey	Slovenia
Asia Pacific	Vanuatu	Malaysia; China; Taiwan*, China	Australia. Japan, Republic of Korea
United States and Western Europe			Belgium, Denmark, Finland, France, Germany, Greece, Iceland, Ireland, Italy, Netherlands, Norway, Portugal, Spain, Sweden, Switzerland, United Kingdom, United States

Source: Kelley, Bosma, and Amorós 2011, 8.
*Indicates an economy in transition to the next stage.

Bosma, and Amorós 2011, 24). Figure 5.1 shows the TEA for the three development stages, comparing the rates in 2009 with those in 2010.

TEA is higher at the early stage of development, *the factor-driven* stage. Efficiency-driven economies show the second-highest rate, and innovation-driven economies the lowest. Among the regions, countries in the Middle East and North Africa and the South Asia regions show relatively lower rates of TEA, while countries in Sub-Saharan Africa show the highest rates. Among the economies in the efficiency-driven group, entrepreneurial activity is highest in Latin America and lowest in Eastern Europe. Entrepreneurial activity in the Asian countries varies, with China showing high levels and Malaysia exhibiting low levels. Western European economies dominate the innovation-driven group, along with the United States and three economies in the Asia-Pacific region. Australia, Iceland, and the United States show the highest rates of TEA.

Plotting TEA against per capita GDP illustrates again the high rate of TEA in factor-driven economies that declines and levels out for the efficiency-driven economies and begins to increase again for the innovation-driven economies. The key reason for this pattern can be found in the *motivation* for entrepreneurship. Acs (2006) describes two types of entrepreneurs, those who become entrepreneurs because of "necessity" and those who are "opportunity" entrepreneurs exploiting a new or latent opportunity. The GEM also uses this classification, which classifies "opportunity" entrepreneurship further into those who "seek to maintain or increase their income" and those who "desire independence in their work" (Kelley, Bosma, and Amorós 2011, 26). Necessity entrepreneurs are to be found among the self-employed. Lacking sufficient employment opportunities, they have no option except to start their own enterprise. Necessity entrepreneurs are higher as a proportion of TEA in developing economies where labor is abundant and job opportunities are scarce. As development progresses, per capita GDP increases, and economies exhibit greater political and macroeconomic stability, employment opportunities emerge in the productive sectors, and necessity entrepreneurship declines. Self-employment rates fall as even marginal managers can earn more money being employed by someone else. Thus, the nature of entrepreneurship changes, and "opportunity" entrepreneurship emerges. As economies enter into the final stages of development, technological change and knowledge-intensive industries become important. Entrepreneurs "have access to entrepreneurial finance, open markets, R&D knowledge and other entrepreneurship-specific framework conditions"[8] (Kelley, Bosma, and Amorós 2011, 26).

Figure 5.1 Percentage of Population Engaged in Early-Stage Entrepreneurial Activity for 59 Economies by Phase of Economic Development, 2010

(percent)

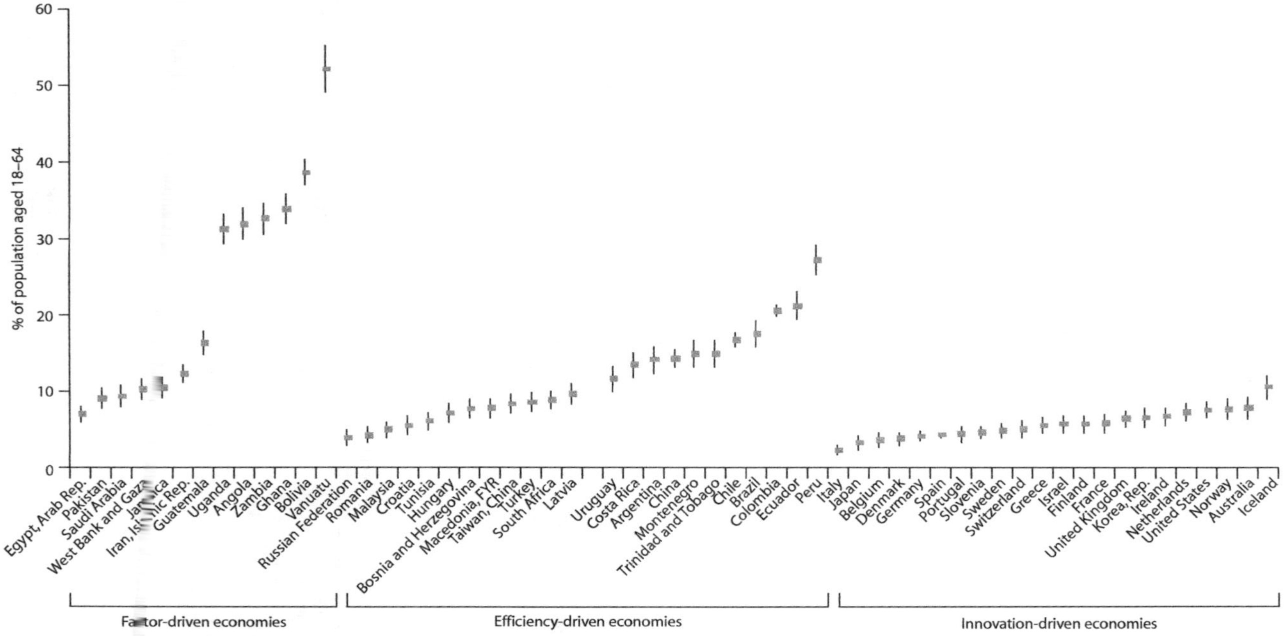

Source: Kelley, Bosma, and Amorós 2011, 24.
Note: Data are at 95 percent confidence intervals.

These factors account for the upward trend of the curve on the right-hand side of figure 5.2.

Two implications may be drawn from the U-shaped graph summarizing the relationship between entrepreneurship and per capita GDP. First, the drop in TEA rates may not always be a cause for concern. In some

Figure 5.2   Percentage of Population Engaged in Total Early-Stage Entrepreneurial Activity by Per Capita GDP, 2010

(percent)

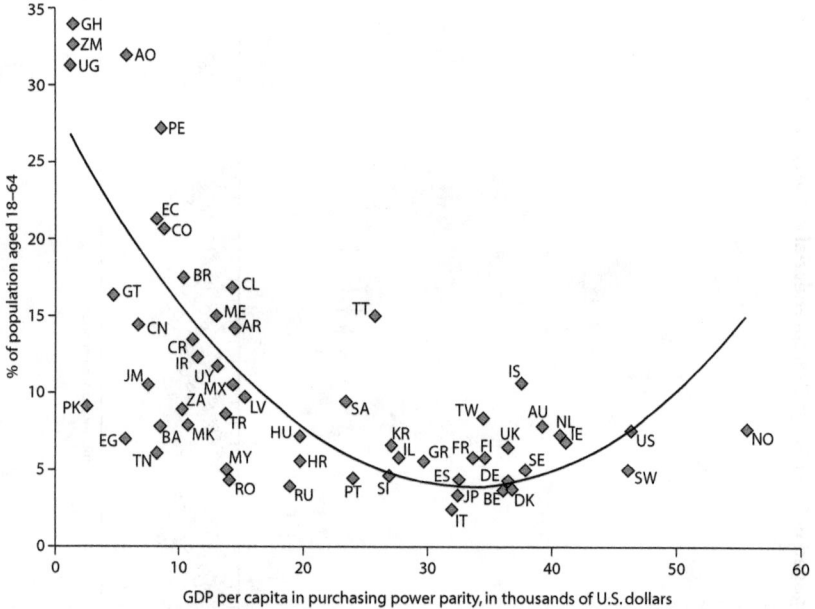

GDP per capita in purchasing power parity, in thousands of U.S. dollars

AO Angola	ES Spain	JP Japan	SA Saudi Arabia
AR Argentina	FI Finland	KR Korea, Rep.	SE Sweden
AU Australia	FR France	LV Latvia	SI Slovenia
BA Bosnia and Herzegovina	GH Ghana	ME Montenegro	SW Switzerland
BE Belgium	GR Greece	MK Macedonia, FYR	TN Tunisia
BR Brazil	GT Guatemala	MX Mexico	TR Turkey
CL Chile	HR Croatia	MY Malaysia	TT Trinidad and Tobago
CN China	HU Hungary	NL Netherlands	TT Taiwan, China
CO Colombia	IE Ireland	NO Norway	UG Uganda
CR Costa Rica	IL Israel	PE Peru	UK United Kingdom
DE Germany	IR Iran, Islamic Rep.	PK Pakistan	US United States
DK Denmark	IS Iceland	PT Portugal	UY Uruguay
EC Ecuador	IT Italy	RO Romania	ZA South Africa
EG Egypt, Arab Rep.	JM Jamaica	RU Russian Federation	ZM Zambia

Source: Kelley, Bosma, and Amorós, 2011, 27.
Note: $R^2 = 0.51$. Bolivia and Vanuatu are not shown because their TEA rates are outliers.

economies, declining necessity entrepreneurship may indicate an improving macroeconomy with increasing job opportunities. It may also suggest a shift toward more innovation, growth, and international trade (Kelley, Bosma, and Amorós 2011), begot by entrepreneurs. Second, the upward trend at higher levels of per capita GDP suggests that promoting a positive environment for entrepreneurship encourages individuals to start their own businesses, even when they have a choice of options for employment.

Gries and Naudé (2010) model entrepreneurial abilities—differentiating between mature and start-up entrepreneurs and between necessity entrepreneurship in the traditional (informal) sector and opportunity-driven entrepreneurship in the modern sector—by considering them a component of human capital. By concentrating on the opportunity-driven entrepreneur in the modern sector, the authors show that this type of entrepreneur drives structural transformation through innovation and provision of intermediate inputs and service, thereby increasing employment and productivity in the modern and traditional sectors (Gries and Naudé 2010, 6).

While the TEA is a prime indicator of a dynamic economy, stability through business continuance and growth is also necessary for an economy to grow and develop. The data compiled by the GEM facilitate a comparison of TEA and established businesses (those in existence for 42 months or longer). From these data, one can ascertain the overall rate of business ownership (high or low) and whether conditions in an economy favor TEA over established businesses or vice versa.

According to the 2010 results, the rate of established businesses outpaces that of TEA as GDP increases: thus, none of the factor-driven economies had a rate of established business greater than TEA, while all but four economies of the innovation-driven group had, as shown in figure 5.3. This finding may reflect greater economic stability among the latter group and "greater sustainability of business activities as per capita GDP increases" (Kelley, Bosma, and Amorós 2011, 36). Failure to grow a business from the TEA stage in factor-driven economies may stem from instability in the economic environment. It behooves policy makers in these economies to get the business environment right. Several findings resulted from the GEM 2010 survey:[9]

- Both TEA and the rate of established business are low in MENA compared to the rest of the factor-driven economies.
- Countries in Sub-Saharan Africa had high TEA rates with divided results for established businesses.

Figure 5.3 Established Entrepreneurial Activity for 59 Economies by Phase of Economic Development, 2010

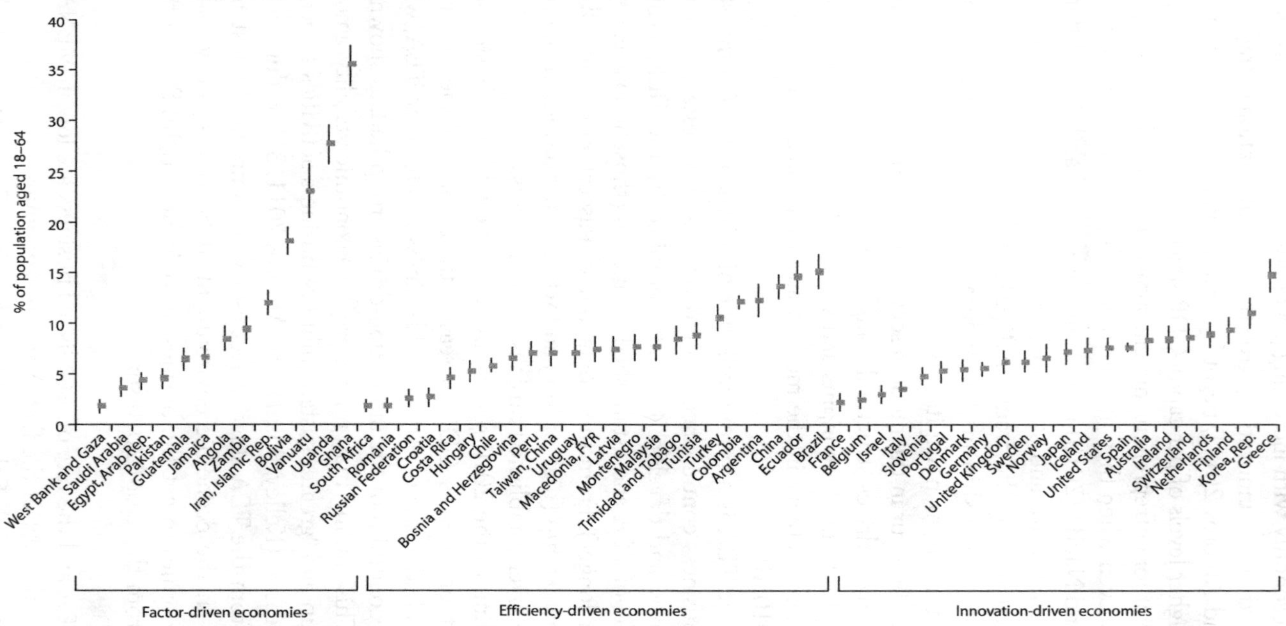

Source: Kelley, Bosma, and Amorós 2011, 36.
Note: Data are at 95 percent confidence intervals.

- Among the efficiency-driven economies, countries in Eastern Europe with low TEA rates showed even lower established business rates, while the scenario in the Latin American countries was mixed: Mexico showed low TEA and nonexistent established businesses, Peru showed high TEA and low established businesses, and Brazil had the highest level of established businesses.
- The rate of established businesses among the innovation-driven economies was higher than the rate of TEA.

The third component of an entrepreneurial dynamic economy is business discontinuance. The GEM surveys those who have discontinued their business in the previous 12 months. The results from the survey show that in the factor-driven group, countries with high TEA also have high discontinuance rates. The relationship between TEA and discontinuance for the efficiency and innovation-driven economies shows a large gap between business start-ups and business closings, on average. Exceptions are the United States, which has high rates of TEA and high rates of discontinuance (Kelley, Bosma, and Amorós 2011, 37).

Entrepreneurship and Job Creation

The previous section summarized the salient features of the entrepreneurial economy while highlighting its links to economic growth and development. This section isolates one of the main components of entrepreneurship, which is that of job creation. Entrepreneurship represents a prime catalyst for employment and for expanding economic opportunities for growth and development. Ghani, Kerr, and O'Connell (2011) examine the relationship between employment growth and entrepreneurship and note the "strong upward slope to the trend line, similar to that found across cities in the United States" (2011, 11) (see figure 5.4).

The GEM survey provides information on the contribution and expected contribution of entrepreneurship to job growth. Some 250 million people were involved in early-stage entrepreneurial activity: nascent entrepreneurs and owner-managers in business for less than 3.5 years. Of these, 55 percent expect to hire between 1 and 5 employees in the coming five years; an estimated 63 million or 25 percent expected to hire at least 5 employees, and 27 million of these expected to hire 20 or more employees in five years. Figure 5.5 presents the data on expectations for job growth for early-stage entrepreneurial activity between 2008 and

Figure 5.4   Entrepreneurship and Growth in Indian Manufacturing, by State, 1989–2005

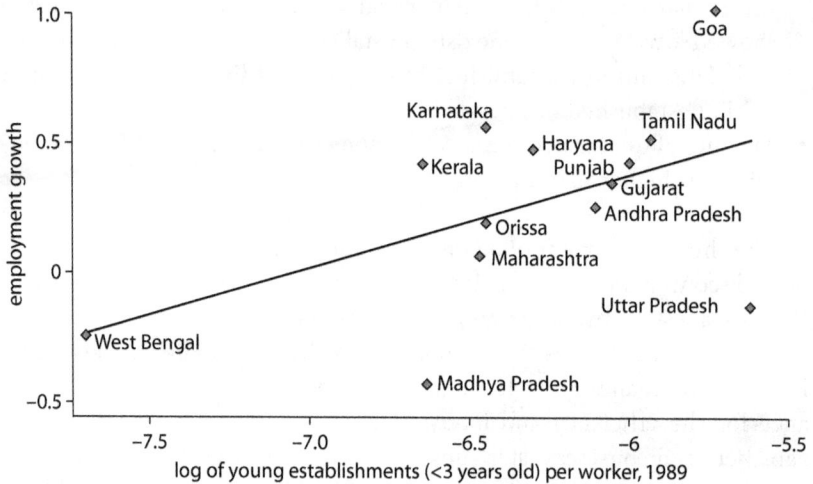

Source: Ghani, Kerr, and O'Connell 2011, 12.
Note: Plotted points represent Indian states of Goa, Gujarat, Haryana, Karnataka, Kerala, Madhya Pradesh, Maharashtra, Orissa, Punjab, Tamil Nadu, Uttar Pradesh, and West Bengal.

2010 by type of economy. The chart also differentiates between entrepreneurship of "moderate-growth expectations" (expected growth between 5 and 19 employees) and that of "high-growth expectations" (expected growth greater than 20 employees). The latter type has been noted to "contribute a disproportionate share of all new jobs created by new firms" (Kelley, Bosma, and Amorós 2011, 40) and is the type that receives attention from policy makers. The 2010 survey found the following:

- The factor-driven economies have a generally lower proportion of high-growth expectations.
- An average of 21 percent of entrepreneurs in the factor-driven economies expect to create 5 or more jobs in five years, while an average of 4.6 percent expect to create 20 or more jobs.
- An average of 29 percent of entrepreneurs in the efficiency-driven economies expect to create 5 or more jobs in five years and an average of 7.1 percent expect to create 20 jobs or more.
- An average of 28 percent of entrepreneurs from the innovation-driven economies expect to create 5 or more jobs, and 7.8 percent of entrepreneurs from this group of countries expect to create 20 or more jobs.

Figure 5.5 Job Growth Expectations for Early-Stage Entrepreneurship Activity, 2008–10

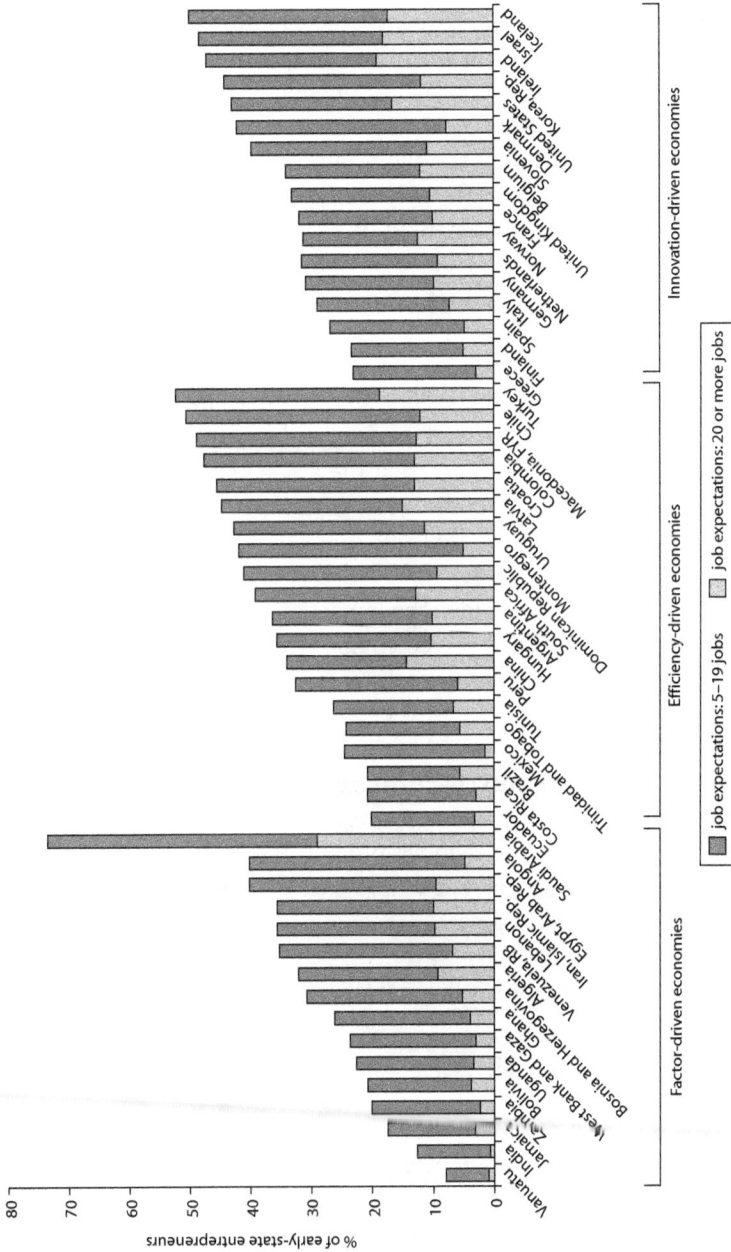

Legend:
- job expectations: 5–19 jobs
- job expectations: 20 or more jobs

y-axis: % of early-state entrepreneurs

Categories: Innovation-driven economies, Efficiency-driven economies, Factor-driven economies

Innovation-driven economies (top to bottom): Iceland, Israel, Korea Rep., Ireland, United States, Denmark, Slovenia, Belgium, United Kingdom, France, Norway, Netherlands, Germany, Italy, Spain, Finland, Greece

Efficiency-driven economies: Turkey, Chile, Colombia, FR Macedonia, Croatia, Latvia, Uruguay, Montenegro, Dominican Republic, South Africa, Argentina, Hungary, China, Peru, Tunisia, Mexico, Brazil, Trinidad and Tobago, Costa Rica

Factor-driven economies: Ecuador, Saudi Arabia, Angola, Egypt, Arab Rep., Iran, Islamic Rep., Lebanon, Venezuela, RB, Algeria, Ghana, Bosnia and Herzegovina, West Bank and Gaza, Uganda, Bolivia, Zambia, Jamaica, India, Vanuatu

Source: Kelley, Bosma, and Amorós 2011, 41.

High-growth entrepreneurship is positively associated with economic growth (Wong, Ho, and Autio 2005; Autio 2008). This type of entrepreneurship is particularly important for developing economies as they strive to catch up in growth and develop their technological and knowledge capabilities. Yet the determinants of high-growth entrepreneurship in developing countries have received relatively little research attention compared to research on the types of entrepreneurship in the advanced economies (Naudé 2010a).[10] Goedhuys and Sleuwaegen (2010) examined high-growth entrepreneurial firms in Sub-Saharan Africa and found that 6 percent of firms from a sample of 954 firms across 11 of the region's countries fell into that category. They estimate an empirical model in which firm growth is a function of initial employment, firm age, entrepreneurial characteristics, technology, institutional resources, and country and industry effects. They also find that firm size, minority entrepreneurs, education level, and product and process innovation determine high-growth expectations and that the availability of transport and transport infrastructure are significant in explaining high-growth potential.

In 2005, the GEM carried out a review of high-growth-expectation entrepreneurial activity. It expanded this review again in 2006 and in 2007.[11] The review examined the impact of entrepreneurial demographics and the characteristics of the economic environment on high-expectation entrepreneurs, high-growth entrepreneurs, entrepreneurs in general, and the general population. High-expectation (those expecting to create 20 or more jobs in five years) and high growth entrepreneurs (those who currently have 20 employees) were categorized as nascent, new, or established entrepreneurs.

The results from the demographic profile that examined age, education, gender, income, current employment status, motivation, and sector suggest several conclusions:

- Nascent high-expectation entrepreneurs are biased toward young individuals.
- Established high-growth entrepreneurs are biased toward older individuals.
- Women are particularly underrepresented among high-expectation and high-growth entrepreneurs.
- High-expectation and high-growth entrepreneurs tend to have more education than entrepreneurs in general; lower levels of education are underrepresented among all entrepreneurs.

- High-expectation and high-growth-expectation entrepreneurs tend to belong to the higher-income brackets: 43 percent of nascent high-expectation entrepreneurs belonged to the highest income tier, and 63 percent of established high-growth entrepreneurs belonged to the highest income tier.
- High-growth and high-expectation entrepreneurs are more likely to have full- or part-time jobs compared to the general population (Autio 2007, 29).
- High-expectation and high-growth entrepreneurs are twice as likely as other entrepreneurs to have made "business angel" investments during the past three years, are more likely to know other entrepreneurs, and are more likely to expect to start a new business within the next three years.
- Nascent and new high-expectation entrepreneurs are less likely to be inhibited by fear of failure, more likely to be optimistic about start-up opportunities, and more likely to believe that they have sufficient skills to start a new firm compared to the general population of entrepreneurs and established high-growth entrepreneurs.
- High-expectation and high-growth entrepreneurs are underrepresented in primary agricultural output.
- New high-expectation and established high-growth entrepreneurs are slightly overrepresented in the manufacturing sector and in transportation, communication, and utilities.
- Nascent high-expectation entrepreneurs are overrepresented in the financial, insurance, and real estate sectors, while high-growth established entrepreneurs are underrepresented in these sectors (Autio 2007).

In summary, education and household income are significantly associated with high-expectation and high-growth entrepreneurs who are more highly represented in the manufacturing and service sectors. High-expectation and high-growth entrepreneurs exhibit a different demographic profile from that of entrepreneurs in general and the general population.

The demographic profile of high-expectation and high growth entrepreneurship does not differ markedly among the various types of identified economies, that is, the factor-driven, the efficiency-driven, and the innovation-driven economy. However, the number of high-growth and high-expectation entrepreneurs differs significantly between low- and middle-income economies and high-income economies. As an economy's per capita income increases, so too does its rate of high-growth entrepreneurship (see figure 5.6). Differences within income groups can also be quite large. The GEM 2007 report (Autio 2007) refers to a five-fold difference between China and India in high-growth and high-expectation entrepreneurship. Similarly, Iceland's rate of high-growth and high-expectation entrepreneurship is three to four times greater than that of Finland. These variations suggest a role for policy. In fact, the educational system may help, especially given the positive role of culture in shaping a society's view of entrepreneurship.

Autio (2007) also examined the effect of national policy on high-growth and high-expectation entrepreneurship and on low-growth entrepreneurship. The facets of policy examined were availability of funding for new and growing firms, government policy priorities on entrepreneurship, degree of regulatory burden, availability and quality of support programs, role of primary and secondary education in promoting entrepreneurial skills, accessibility and quality of a national science and technology base for new and growing firms, availability and accessibility of

Figure 5.6   The Relationship between Per Capita GDP and High-Growth Entrepreneurship, 2003–08

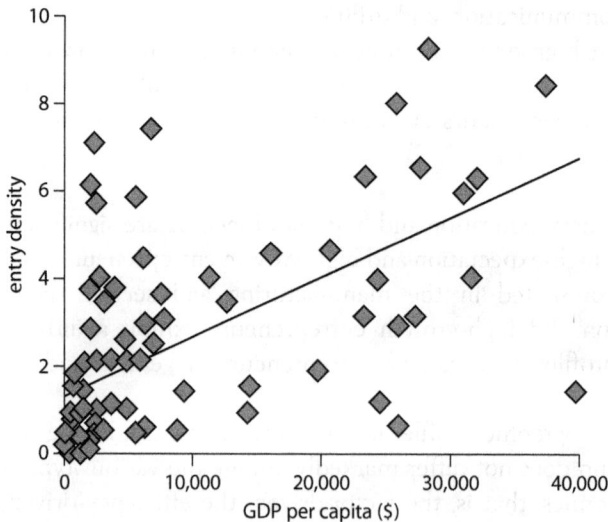

Source: Klapper and Love 2010, 10.
Note: Entry density refers to the number of newly registered limited-liability firms in the corresponding year as a percentage of the country's working-age population (aged 15–65) normalized by 1,000. GDP data are for 2009.

business services, dynamism and change in consumer markets, ease of market entry, quality of physical infrastructure, and protection of intellectual property rights. The study came to several conclusions:

- Overall entrepreneurial activity is either negatively (significantly) or neutrally (insignificantly) associated with national policy conditions influencing entrepreneurship.
- New and established entrepreneurial activity is positively and significantly associated with domestic market change and dynamism.
- High-growth, high-expectation entrepreneurship is positively correlated with the following:
  - Government regulations
  - Education support for entrepreneurship
  - Market openness
  - Physical infrastructure
  - Intellectual property rights protection (for established high-growth entrepreneurship).
- High-growth, high-expectation entrepreneurship is negatively correlated with domestic market change and dynamism (Autio 2007).

Autio (2007) cautions about making inferences from these results. First, he notes that the correlations for overall entrepreneurial activity may be explained by the fact that "overall levels of entrepreneurial activity tend to be higher in middle-to-low income countries, where the policy framework and business infrastructure may not be as well developed as it is in high income countries" (Autio 2007, 35). Furthermore, the positive correlations found for high-growth and high-expectation entrepreneurship may be explained by the greater levels of high-growth and high-expectation entrepreneurship in high-income countries. Economic wealth rather than policy may be driving the correlations. The main conclusion is that overall entrepreneurship and high-growth, high-expectation entrepreneurship differ from one another when it comes to national policy. Moreover, policy aimed at overall levels of entrepreneurship may stymie high-growth entrepreneurship. Increasing the number of entrepreneurs does not mean that high-growth entrepreneurship will follow. Policy needs to be mindful of both quality and quantity in its design.

The roles of social and cultural frameworks in promoting entrepreneurship were also considered. Both overall entrepreneurship and high-growth, high-expectation entrepreneurship were positively linked with national culture and social framework conditions (Autio 2007).[12]

Female Entrepreneurship

Women entrepreneurs make an important contribution to economic development, particularly in low- and middle-income countries. The research on women in development notes that women are more likely than men to share their gains in education, health, and microfinance with members of their families and the community at large.[13] Investment in female entrepreneurship is one further way to achieve stronger economic growth and development (Minniti 2010, 294).[14] The following sections examine some key aspects of female entrepreneurship that have implications for policy and for maximizing the development role of women entrepreneurs. Empowering women in entrepreneurship by directing a range of initiatives toward the female entrepreneur is becoming more common in developing economies. Part of the reason stems from the positive results from the research on women in development and also the positive role that entrepreneurship itself makes to economic growth and development.

Gender Gap in Entrepreneurship

The rate of business ownership and management of businesses is higher for men than women, creating a "gender gap" in entrepreneurship.[15] Businesses are more likely to be owned by men and tend to be larger than those owned by women (OECD 1998; Thurik and Verheul 2001; Valenzuela 2004; Terjesen and Amorós 2010). Furthermore, large gender gaps exist with regard to start-up activity (Minniti 2009). One of the main aspects examined by Allen, Elam, Langowitz, and Dean (2008b) in their study of the role of women in entrepreneurship was that of a gender gap in venture creation and ownership activity (see table 5.2).[16]

Table 5.2   Gender Gap in Venture Creation and Ownership Activity, 2007

(percent)

Economies	Early stage	Established
Low and middle income		
Europe and Asia	44.8	44.3
Latin America and the Caribbean	24.0	47.1
High income	43.4	52.3

Source: Allen, Elam, Langowitz, and Dean 2008b.

Allen, Elam, Langowitz, and Dean (2008b) noted that in the countries they studied, men were more likely than women to be involved in entrepreneurial activity, with the exceptions of Brazil, Japan, Peru, and Thailand.[17] Table 5.2 presents the data. The gender gap is greatest among high-income countries (those with an average per capita income close to US$35,000 and average GDP growth of 3.5 percent) for both early-stage and established business ownership. Low- and middle-income economies in Europe and Asia (those with an average per capita income of US$10,407) had similar gaps. Only in the low- and middle-income economies of Latin America and the Caribbean is the gender gap smaller, but for early-stage activity only. The gender gap for established ownership is in line with that of other low- and middle-income economies in Europe and Asia and of high-income economies.

Table 5.3 shows the large proportion of women entrepreneurs in the low- and middle-income economies of Latin America and the Caribbean compared to that in the high-income countries. In both of the low- and middle-income groupings, women entrepreneurs are more prevalent in early-stage entrepreneurial activity. Chamlee-Wright (1997) showed that entrepreneurship in Ghana is a way out of poverty for women with fewer opportunities in formal labor markets. The likelihood of business survivorship in the low- and middle-income countries is higher for men than for women, although there is no discernible gender difference in business survival in the high-income countries. Furthermore, the evolution from early-stage entrepreneurial activity to established business is more likely in the high-income countries.

Table 5.3   Entrepreneurial Activity by Gender and Type across Country Groups, 2007

(percent)

	Early-stage entrepreneurial activity (nascent + new)		Established business owners		All business owners (nascent + new + established)	
	Male	Female	Male	Female	Male	Female
Low- and middle-income countries in Europe and Asia	11.70	7.62	8.19	4.02	19.89	12.24
Low- and middle-income countries in Latin America and the Caribbean	19.55	14.40	12.21	6.57	31.76	20.97
High-income countries	8.17	4.34	7.91	3.57	16.08	7.91

Source: Allen, Elam, Langowitz and Dean (2008a) 14.
Note: Significant difference between country clusters for all business categories = p <0.0001.

Allen, Elam, Langowitz, and Dean (2008a) also note a gender gap in the motivation for entrepreneurship. Table 5.4 compares gender differences for *opportunity* and *necessity* entrepreneurship. The ratio of opportunity to necessity entrepreneurship is highest for the high-income countries for both sexes. Evidence of a gender gap in opportunity entrepreneurship exists across all income groups, whereas no gender gap is evident for necessity entrepreneurship. Moreover, Minniti (2009) found that the gender gap in start-up activity is much larger in middle-income countries than in low-income countries, a fact she attributes to a greater incidence of necessity entrepreneurship in the latter. A recent report on female entrepreneurship in the Latin America and Caribbean region notes that women are more likely to experience "push-out factors" that are derived from necessity entrepreneurship (World Bank 2010). Examples include asset and human capital accumulation, child care responsibilities, and intrahousehold allocation of resources. "Pull-in factors," which are associated with opportunity-based entrepreneurship, are more often associated with males. The report identifies these as "often based on the desire for flexibility, following a life's calling, innate ability, starting or joining in a family business and identifying a unique business opportunity" (World Bank 2010, 10).

Answers to questions about why women entrepreneurs are more likely to cluster in early-stage entrepreneurial activity and are less successful than their male counterparts at staying in business beyond 42 months are necessary in understanding female entrepreneurship. Demographic characteristics shed light on these questions, as does the economic environment.

Table 5.4   Country Group Differences in Opportunity and Necessity Early-Stage Entrepreneurship by Gender, 2007

	Opportunity entrepreneurship		Necessity entrepreneurship		Opportunity-to-necessity ratio	
	Male	Female	Male	Female	Male	Female
Low- and middle-income countries in Europe and Asia	7.35	4.35	4.50	2.22	1.63	1.96
Low- and middle-income countries in Latin America and the Caribbean	12.38	7.51	7.51	5.33	1.65	1.41
High-income countries	6.85	3.56	1.18	0.83	5.81	4.28

Source: Allen, Elam, Langowitz, and Dean 2008a, 21.

Demographic Characteristics and Economic Environment

Both demographics and the economic environment affect the decision to start a business. Age, education, work status, income, social ties, and perceptions are among the demographic and economic characteristics studied. Differences are visible between female entrepreneurs among the country groups, with little discernible difference between the sexes.[18] Minniti notes that "over time, most scholars have converged on similar views and now agree that some objectively measureable characteristics and some subjective perceptions are all significantly correlated to entrepreneurship" (2010, 297).[19] Data from Allen, Elam, Langowitz, and Dean (2008a) identify several demographic and economic characteristics of female entrepreneurs:

* The age at which women entrepreneurs start a business is broadly similar to that for males. The majority of early-stage businesses are formed when the entrepreneur is aged 25–34, and for established businesses between the ages of 35 and 44. Moreover, the findings are comparable across the country groups, although the age profile is slightly longer for the high-income countries: early-stage female entrepreneurship occurs between the ages of 25 and 44 and established entrepreneurship occurs between the ages of 35 and 55.

* The educational level of female entrepreneurs is also higher in high-income countries, where more than half of female entrepreneurs have secondary degrees and more than one-quarter have graduate degrees. There is no discernible difference between the educational levels of male and female entrepreneurs or for female early-stage and female established entrepreneurship (see table 5.5).

* One exception is employment, for which there are no gender or country differences in entrepreneurship: "The likelihood of being involved in entrepreneurial activity is three to four times higher for those women who also are employed in a wage job (whether full or part time) compared to those who are not working, are retired, or are students" (Allen, Elam, Langowitz, and Dean 2008b, 3).

* As income increases, so too does entrepreneurial activity for women in both early-stage and established businesses in high-income countries (see figure 5.7). Female early-stage entrepreneurial activity in the low- and middle-income countries of Latin America and the Caribbean is four times higher than that in the high-income countries and twice as

Table 5.5 Female Educational Attainments by Country Group and Business Stage, 2007

(percent)

Country grouping	Some secondary		Secondary degree		Post secondary		Graduate experience	
	Early stage	*Established*	*Early stage*	*Established*	*Early stage*	*Established*	*Early stage*	*Established*
Low- and middle-income Europe and Asia	39.2	39.7	24.6	25.1	16.8	17.5	19.4	17.7
Low- and middle-income Latin America and the Caribbean	34.1	40.4	32.1	29.4	23.4	18.8	10.4	11.4
High income	21.6	28.2	28.4	28.1	21.6	14.8	28.4	28.8

Source: Compiled from Allen, Elam, Langowitz, and Dean 2008a, 30.

Figure 5.7 Household Income of Women Entrepreneurs by Country Group and Business Stage, 2007

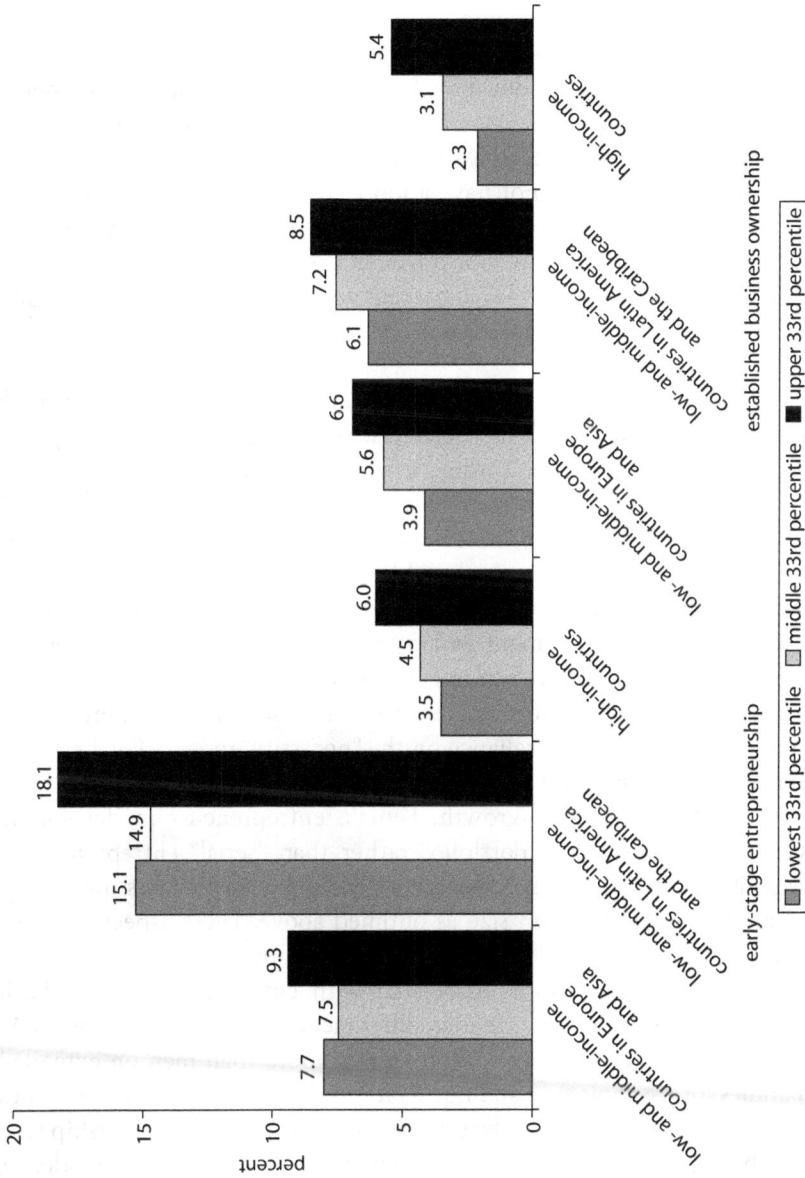

Source: Allen, Elam, Langowitz, and Dean 2008a, 31.

high as such activity in the low- and middle-income countries of Europe and Asia.

- For low- and middle-income economies, having a job is a better indicator of female early-stage entrepreneurship than either household income or secondary education. For example, for female entrepreneurs in the lowest-percentile income group, having a job makes them more than three times more likely to be involved in early-stage entrepreneurship than if they do not have a job (74.3 percent and 21.6 percent, respectively). Given some secondary education, a woman with a job is nearly twice as likely to be involved in early-stage entrepreneurship as a woman without a job (17.6 percent versus 9.9 percent) (Allen, Elam, Langowitz, and Dean 2008a).

A special edition of the *Economic Journal for Development Research* (2010) examined variables associated with female entrepreneurship and whether these changed according to gender or a country's stage of economic development.[20] In summarizing the results, Minniti and Naudé (2010) refer to a higher prevalence of female entrepreneurship in developing economies, a fact attributable to the higher barriers to entry women face in formal labor markets. Women enter entrepreneurship to escape from unemployment and poverty. In fact, up to 35 percent of women in Peru were involved in entrepreneurship (Terjesen and Amorós 2010). The motivation for female entrepreneurship in developing economies indicates a greater reliance on the "necessity" motive. Furthermore, female entrepreneurs in developing economies are more concerned with firm survival than firm growth. Female entrepreneurs in developing economies tend to be "portfolio" rather than "serial" entrepreneurs.[21] Minniti and Naudé (2010) identify a gender gap in business ownership, start-up activity, and firm size as outlined above. These aspects are also similar to entrepreneurship in developed economies.

Some subjective factors associated with entrepreneurship for both men and women exhibit gender differences. Women entrepreneurs in developed and developing economies rely more than men on extended families for psychological and financial support. Minniti (2010) identifies three groups of perceptual factors associated with entrepreneurship that exhibit gender differences: perceptions of opportunity, self-confidence, and fear of failure. Using data from the 2004 GEM, she shows that such perceptions differ significantly between men and women (see table 5.6), even though the "distribution of answers by women follows qualitatively that of men across all income groups."

Table 5.6   Differences between Men and Women in Three Subjective Factors Associated with Entrepreneurship
(percent)

	Self-confidence		Fear of failure		Recognition of opportunities for entrepreneurship	
	Men	*Women*	*Men*	*Women*	*Men*	*Women*
Total sample	58	41	33	40	41	33

Source: Minniti 2010, 302.
Note: Gender differences in perceptions are significant at >99 percent confidence according to a Chi^2-test for all categories.

Men rate their skills, experience, and knowledge much higher (17-percentage-point difference) than women do and also their ability to recognize opportunities for entrepreneurship (8-percentage-point difference). Furthermore, men's fear of failure is significantly lower than women's. Minniti notes that perceptions are subjective and may not reflect the "objective capacity" of the person in question (2010, 302). She investigates whether differences hold when the statistical technique known as "bootstrapping"[22] is used to equalize the data for men and women. Her findings suggest that when the data are equalized for men and women, economic and demographic factors (age, household income, work status, and education) do not seem to be significantly associated with gender. The country context and perceptual variables, however, "seem to account for much of the difference in gender propensity with respect to starting a business" (Minniti 2010, 306).

Factor Markets and Female Entrepreneurship

Labor markets play an important part both in stimulating entrepreneurship and in benefiting from entrepreneurship. Regarding the stimulating aspect, female entrepreneurs who had a job were three to four times more likely to enter into early-stage entrepreneurial activity than those who did not have a job. One of the reasons advanced by the GEM for this is that "working may provide access to resources, social capital, and ideas that may aid in establishing an entrepreneurial venture" (Allen, Elam, Langowitz, and Dean 2008a, 29). Figure 5.8 examines female early-stage entrepreneurship activity by work status and country groups. Low- and middle-income countries in Latin America and the Caribbean show a much larger proportion of females engaging in early-stage entrepreneurial activity than the other two country groupings, likely reflecting the higher incidence of necessity entrepreneurship in the region. The GEM notes

Figure 5.8   Female Early-Stage Entrepreneurial Activity by Work Status and Country Groups, 2007

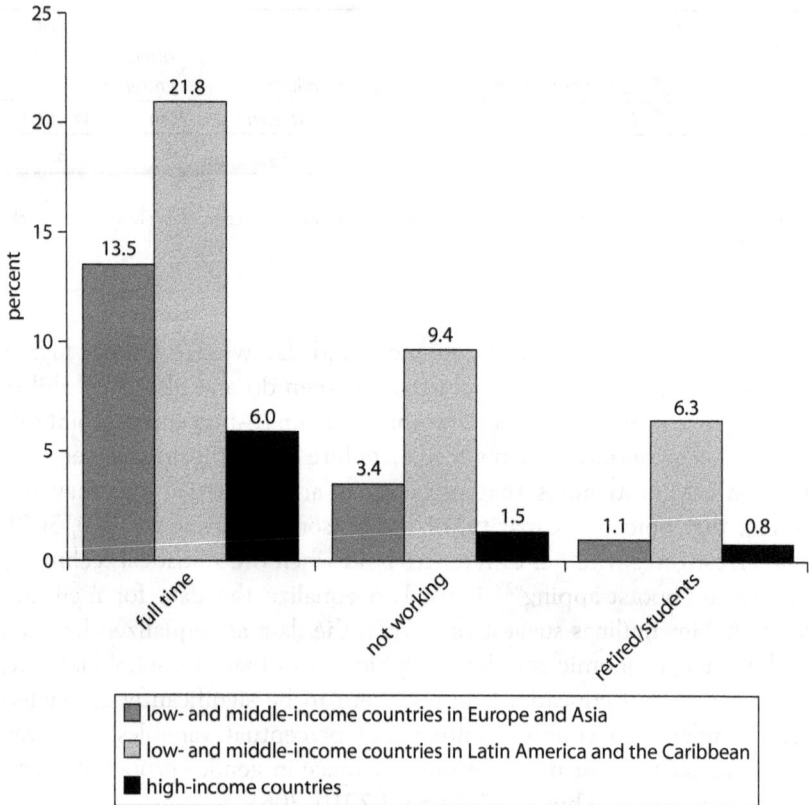

Source: Allen, Elam, Langowitz, and Dean 2008a, 29.

that the difference across countries is not statistically significant, either for the early-stage entrepreneurial activity or the established business owners (Allen, Elam, Langowitz, and Dean 2008a).

As noted by the GTZ–World Bank–Inter-American Development Bank (IDB) report[23] on entrepreneurship in Latin America and the Caribbean, however, lack of opportunities in the formal labor markets influences the decision to become an entrepreneur, in particular for poor women and those who become microenterprise owners. The pool of women in informal markets across many of the countries in Latin America and the Caribbean is significantly higher than that of their male counterparts (see figures 5.9 and 5.10).

Figure 5.9 Percentage of Women Employed in Latin America and the Caribbean, 2009

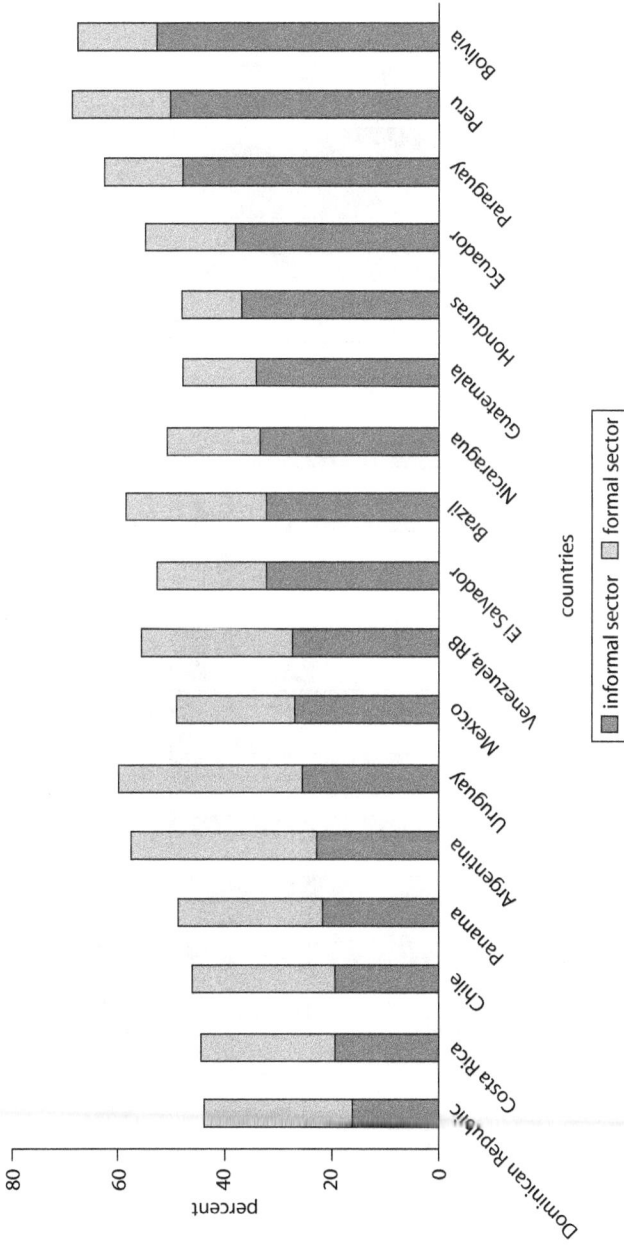

Source: GTZ, World Bank and IDB 2010, 17.

Figure 5.10 Percentage of Men Employed in Latin America and the Caribbean, 2009

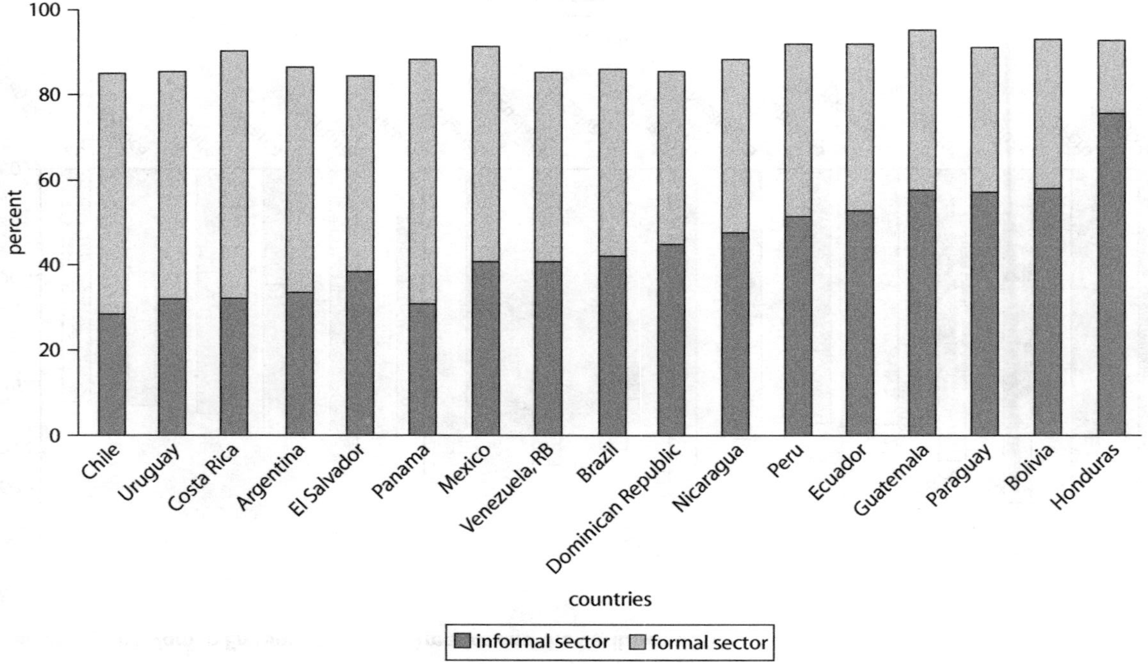
100
80
60
40
20
0
percent
Chile
Uruguay
Costa Rica
Argentina
El Salvador
Panama
Mexico
Venezuela, RB
Brazil
Dominican Republic
Nicaragua
Peru
Ecuador
Guatemala
Paraguay
Bolivia
Honduras
countries
informal sector
formal sector

Source: GTZ, World Bank, and IDB 2010, 17.

One of the reasons advanced for why female-owned enterprises prove less profitable than male-owned enterprises is access to finance. Table 5.7 examines the various providers of finance for micro and small enterprises.

The gender gap in the factor market for finance is one of the central issues examined in the empirical literature on women entrepreneurs and finance. This literature is quite slim in the developing-economy context and largely confined to case studies, which makes it difficult to draw robust conclusions, given the specificity of the data on time and place. Furthermore, a gender gap in access to finance is difficult to isolate from gender differences in other related issues such as the use of formal and informal finance, collateral, intrahousehold relations, education, titling, and credit history. Gender differences in these issues are more likely to affect access to finance rather than indicate any overt discrimination in the factor market for finance.[24] Culture, religion, and the legal environment also affect a woman's ability to access finance (Nallari and Griffith 2011) as well as the type of enterprise being operated.

Indeed, a recent study by Aterido, Beck, and Iacovone (2011) concluded that "there was limited evidence of a gender gap for either households or enterprises" in access to formal finance by female entrepreneurs in Sub-Saharan Africa. The reasons extended beyond the factor market for formal finance and were primarily associated with the type of enterprises and the demographics of the households. According to the study,

Table 5.7   Sources and Nature of Finance for Micro and Small Enterprises, 2005

Source	Nature of financing
Informal	Financing from family and friends, supplier credit, and commercial moneylenders
Semiformal	Rotating savings and credit associations
Nongovernmental organization	Donor funds provided to nongovernmental organizations for distribution to qualifying micro and small enterprises
Microfinance institution	Delivery of financial services (such as microloans, microsavings accounts, microinsurance, and money transfers) to a large number of productive but resource-poor people in rural and urban areas in a cost-effective and sustainable way
Commercial bank	Uncertain capacity to deal with micro and small enterprise financing. Commercial banks are usually not willing to lend small amounts. A very low proportion of informal business sector operators have access to commercial banks.

Source: ILO 2005a, 26.

- Women are more likely to use informal finance.
- Female ownership is not associated with less access to external finance.
  - Formal female entrepreneurs are a select group; the gap arises "before" entry.
    - Females are less likely to be the sole proprietor.
    - Female-owned businesses tend to be smaller.
    - Female-owned businesses are "more" innovative.
    - Females are less likely to operate in sectors "more dependent" on finance.
- Females score lower in key attributes such as education, formal employment, and being head of households, which, in turn, are key to accessing formal finance.

The joint report of the World Bank and the IDB notes that for microenterprises in Bolivia, Peru, and a group comprising Brazil, Ecuador, El Salvador, Guatemala, Honduras, and Nicaragua, "there are no significant differences in access to credit between men and women" (see figure 5.11).

Enterprise survey data examined by the GTZ–World Bank–IDB report suggest, instead, that male and female entrepreneurs use credit differently. Female entrepreneurs tend to use credit less often, have smaller loans, and rely more frequently on informal sources of credit. Figure 5.12 examines the percentage of entrepreneurs with a loan by size of business and gender for Guatemala. Female entrepreneurs who are self-employed or who employ between two and four employees are significantly less likely to have a loan than their male counterparts. As firm size increases, so does the recourse to loans.

In Bolivia, female entrepreneurs are about 12 percent less likely to have a loan from a financial institution than their male entrepreneurs. They are 16 percent more likely to participate in a rotating savings and credit association. Data on participation in such associations in Kenya show that 76 percent of clients are women (ILO 2005a, 23). The Mexican data quoted in the joint report of the World Bank and the IDB indicated that male entrepreneurs had been 2.1 times more likely to apply for a loan in the previous 12 months than their female counterparts. When asked why they were less likely to apply for a loan, female entrepreneurs most often cited a preference for working with their own resources[25] and also that they perceived discrimination from loan officers. The latter reason is also one cited by female entrepreneurs in Ethiopia, Kenya, and Tanzania (ILO 2005a, 2005b, and 2005c).[26]

Figure 5.11   Bank Financing for Male- and Female-Owned Microenterprises in Bolivia and Peru and Results of Enterprise Surveys, 2003, 2007, and 2008

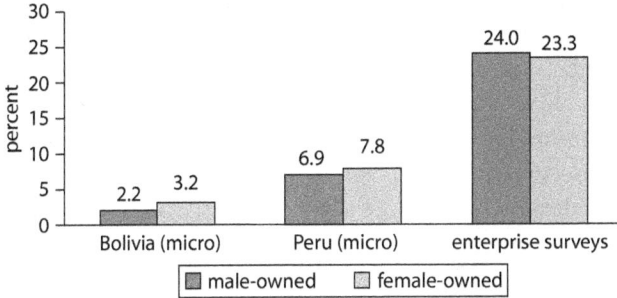

Source: GTZ, World Bank, and IDB 2010, 46, citing World Bank 2005a, 2005b, 2005c, 2007.

Figure 5.12   Percentage of Male and Female Entrepreneurs in Guatemala with a Loan by Size of Business, 2006

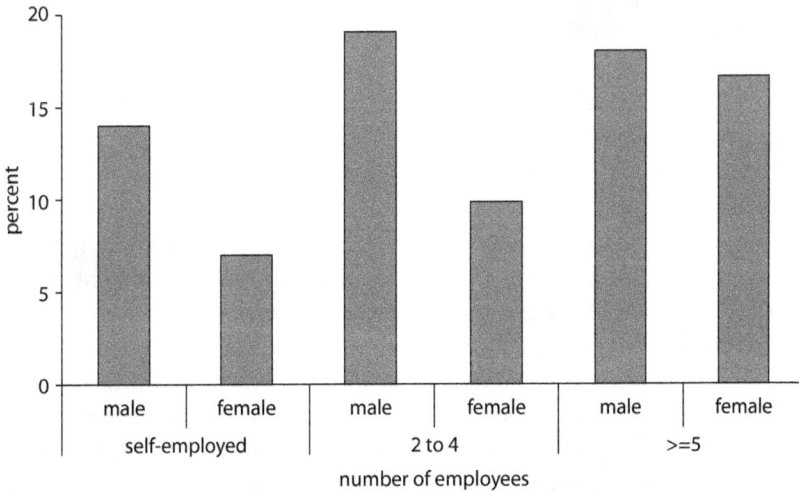

Source: GTZ, World Bank, and IDB 2010, 47.

Conclusion

Using data from the most recent Global Entrepreneurship Monitor, the chapter examined entrepreneurship from the perspectives of economic growth and development, job creation, and female entrepreneurship and supplemented the findings with empirical studies from the literature on entrepreneurship.

Entrepreneurship makes a positive contribution to economic growth and development and vice versa. The main conduit is through the process of structural transformation. The chapter shows the relationship between GDP and entrepreneurship in three phases, representing three phases of development. In countries with low GDP—corresponding to a traditional, agrarian society—entrepreneurship flourishes and represents an alternative to unemployment, providing job opportunities and potential for enterprise creation. The type of entrepreneurship at this level of income and development is primarily "necessity" entrepreneurship. Total early-stage entrepreneurial activity that includes nascent enterprises and those in business for 42 months or less is very high at this stage of development compared to the other stages. As per capita income increases and economies develop, larger and more established firms provide ample job opportunities and satisfy demand in the marketplace; thus, entrepreneurship declines, particularly necessity entrepreneurship. Entrepreneurship in this second phase, which was termed the "efficiency" phase in the chapter, is opportunity entrepreneurship. Individuals become entrepreneurs by choice, exploiting an opportunity they see in the marketplace. The total entrepreneurship activity in relation to per capita GDP declines in this development phase. This decline may not be a cause for concern: individuals who were entrepreneurs by necessity may have found jobs in the formal economy or may indeed have contributed to innovation and international trade, accounting for the rise in per capita GDP. As per capita income increases further and well-developed factor markets for research and development, finance, and institutions support enterprise creation, individuals see greater opportunities, particularly in the technological and knowledge industries; thus, entrepreneurship begins to increase once more. This phase, identified as the 'innovation" phase in the chapter, is dominated by Western European economies, the United States, and three economies in the Asia-Pacific region. The rate of established businesses increases as per capita GDP rises. On average, business discontinuance is highest among the factor-driven economies compared with large gaps between the efficiency-driven and innovation-driven economies.

Entrepreneurship is a prime catalyst for job creation, and there is evidence of a strong upward trend line between entrepreneurship and employment growth. While some entrepreneurs do not aspire to create jobs, others carry "high expectations" of job growth. The latter is particularly important for the developing economies as they strive to catch up with the developed economies in growth, technology, and knowledge. However, high-expectation entrepreneurship is lowest among the factor-driven economies. High-expectation entrepreneurship (defined in the GEM as "moderate" where entrepreneurs expect to create at least 5 jobs and "high" where entrepreneurs expect to create in excess of 20 jobs over five years) has received little research attention compared to high-expectation entrepreneurship in advanced economies. Of the studies that have been carried out, the reasons for high-expectation entrepreneurship are similar in both contexts and center on demographics, economic environment, and country and social context. The demographic profile of high-expectation entrepreneurs differs from that of all entrepreneurs and the general population. Education and household income are significantly associated with high-expectation entrepreneurs, who are more highly represented in the manufacturing and service sectors. The role of policy in promoting entrepreneurship was considered, and the discussion concluded that the policy needs to be mindful of both quantity and quality of entrepreneurship in its design. Furthermore, it is difficult to extrapolate the positive impact of policy on entrepreneurship. Policy needs to be cognizant of the differences between high-growth entrepreneurship and entrepreneurs in general.

Finally, the chapter examined female entrepreneurship, noting its positive contribution to economic development. The chapter examined the gender gap in entrepreneurship that is readily visible in the lower numbers of female entrepreneurs in firm start-up and business ownership. The gender gap is greatest in the high-income economies and for "opportunity" entrepreneurship; there is no gap between men and women in "necessity" entrepreneurship. For many women in developing countries, entrepreneurship represents a way out of poverty. Furthermore, women are more likely to be involved in early-stage entrepreneurial activity and are less likely to stay in business beyond three and a half years. Demographic characteristics of female entrepreneurship are similar to those of males but differ across country groups classified by income level. There is, however, a gender gap in the subjective perceptions related to starting a business that does not differ across country groups. Women are more likely to fear failure and to rate their skills and experience lower than those of males. Thus, the country context (low income, middle income, and high income) and subjective perceptions appear to account for the gender gap in entrepreneurship. The evidence for a gender gap in finance is not supported by the empirical studies. Gender differences in regard to the use of formal and informal credit, collateral, titling, and credit history, however, do come into play. These differences are sometimes confused with a gender gap in finance.

Notes

1. The term *creative destruction* was popularized by Schumpeter (1942).

2. Gries and Naudé (2010) reference Acs, Desai, and Hessels (2008); Acs and Szerb (2009); Amorós, Cristi, and Naudé (2010); Gries and Naudé (2009); Minniti and Naudé (2010); Naudé (2007, 2008, 2009, 2010a, 2010b, 2010c); Naudé, Gries, Wood, and Meintjes (2008) as contributors to the literature on entrepreneurship and development.

3. Institutions pertaining to property rights, rule of law, accountability, good governance, and contract enforcement affect the level of entrepreneurship in the economy.

4. The Global Entrepreneurship Monitor completed its first annual survey of entrepreneurial attitudes, activities, and aspirations of entrepreneurs from 10 developed economies in 1999. Since then, the GEM has expanded and now includes over 80 countries. It has carried out 12 annual surveys since 1999.

5. Kelley, Bosma, and Amorós (2011).

6. See Naudé (2010a) and Leff (1979).

7. According to Lewis, as development proceeds, surplus labor is transferred from rural areas, where its marginal product is zero, to urban areas where its marginal product is positive. This brings about a structural transformation in the economy in which it moves from an agricultural basis to a manufacturing and service basis.

8. The framework conditions refer to entrepreneurial finance, government policy, government entrepreneurship programs, entrepreneurship education, R&D transfer, internal market openness, physical infrastructure for entrepreneurship, commercial and legal infrastructure for entrepreneurship, and cultural and social norms.

9. Authors are Kelley, Bosma, and Amorós (2011).

10. Nyström (2008), who reviewed 38 studies of entrepreneurship and economic performance between 1996 and 2006, found that all but three studies focused on advanced economies (Naudé 2010a, 7).

11. The 2007 report was written by Autio and is discussed here.

12. These were identified as entrepreneurial orientation in national culture; existence of new business opportunities; existence of entrepreneurial skills and capabilities in the population; existence of entrepreneurial motivations in the population; and societal support for female entrepreneurship (Allen, Elam, Langowitz, and Dean 2008a, 34).

13. The Gender Mainstreaming Program, established in 1997 by the United Nations Economic and Social Council, "guides research, policy-making and program development under the United Nations Development Program" (Allen, Elam, Langowitz, and Dean 2008a, 61).

14. "Boserup (1970), for example, highlighted the intense activity of women as entrepreneurs in rural settings in developing countries. The Grameen Bank and other similar initiatives worldwide provide evidence to suggest the importance of female entrepreneurship in poverty reduction (Yunus 2007)," (Minniti 2010, 294–95).

15. On the other hand, "the rate of new business formation by women has outpaced significantly the rate of new business formation by men across all ethnic groups in the United States. Similar trends have been found across the developing world" (Minniti and Naudé 2010, 277).

16. The GEM study used data from 41 countries whose economies represented more than 70 percent of the world's population and 93 percent of global GDP in 2007.

17. Minniti (2010, 295) references Devine (1994a, 1994b), Georgellis and Wall (2005), and Kim (2007) for documenting women's lower propensity for entrepreneurship worldwide compared to men.

18. An exception is that women's optimism and self-esteem about starting a business are lower than those of their male counterparts. Fear of failure was also higher for women compared to men.

19. Minniti (2010, 297) references the contributions of Evans and Jovanovic (1989), Arenius and Minniti (2005), and Minniti and Nardone (2007) for this statement.

20. *European Journal of Development Research*, 22(3) special section, "Female Entrepreneurship across Countries and in Development," edited by Maria Minniti and Wim Naudé, http://www.palgrave-journals.com/ejdr/journal/v22/n3/index.html.

21. Portfolio and serial entrepreneurs are subdivisions of habitual entrepreneurs. The latter refers to individuals who hold or have held a minority or majority ownership stake in two or more businesses, at least one of which was established or purchased. Portfolio entrepreneurs refer to those who currently have minority or majority stakes in two or more independent businesses. Serial entrepreneurs are those who have sold or closed at least one business in which they have had a minority or a majority ownership stake and currently have a minority or a majority ownership stake in a single independent business (Ucbasaran, Alsos, Westhead, and Wright 2008).

22. Bootstrapping is the practice of estimating properties of an estimator (such as its variance) by measuring those properties when sampling from an approximating distribution. One standard choice for an approximating distribution is the empirical distribution of the observed data. In the case where a set of observations can be assumed to be from an independent and identically distributed population, this can be implemented by constructing a number of resamples of the observed dataset (and of equal size to the observed dataset), each of which is obtained by random sampling with replacement from the original dataset. It may also be used for constructing hypothesis tests. It is

often used as an alternative to inference based on parametric assumptions when those assumptions are in doubt, or where parametric inference is impossible or requires very complicated formulas for the calculation of standard errors. See "statistics," http://en.wikipedia.org/wiki/Bootstrapping.

23. Deutsche Gesellschaft für Technische Zusammenarbeit (GTZ) GmbH.

24. See Nallari and Griffith (2011) for references.

25. The report found that savings were more likely to be used by self-employed and small female-led enterprises.

26. The gender gap for loan application and perception of discrimination diminishes for firm size.

References

Acs, Z. 2006. "How Is Entrepreneurship Good for Economic Growth?" *Innovations* 1 (1): 97–107.

Acs, Z. J., S. Desai, and J. Hessels. 2008. "Entrepreneurship, Economic Development and Institutions." *Small Business Economics* 31(3): 219–34.

Acz, Z., and L. Szerb. 2009. "The Global Entrepreneurship Index." *Foundations and Trends in Entrepreneurship* 5 (5): 341–435.

Allen, I. E., A. Elam, N. Langowitz, and M. Dean. 2008a. *The 2007 Global Entrepreneurship Monitor Special Topic Report: Women in Entrepreneurship.* Babson Park, MA: Center for Women's Leadership, Babson College, http://www.gemconsortium.org.

————. 2008b. *The 2007 Global Entrepreneurship Monitor Special Topic Report: Women in Entrepreneurship: Summary Report.* Babson Park, MA: Center for Women's Leadership, Babson College, http://www.gemconsortium.org.

Amorós, E., O. Cristi, and W. A. Naudé. 2010. "Romanticizing Penniless Entrepreneurs? Poverty, Vulnerability, Non-Monetary Welfare and Business Start-Up Rates across Countries." Paper prepared for the Babson College Entrepreneurship Research Conference, Lausanne, Switzerland, June 9–12.

Arenius, P., and M. Minniti. 2005. "Perceptual Variables and Nascent Entrepreneurship." *Small. Business Economics* 24 (3): 233–47.

Aterido, R., T. Beck, and L. Iavocone. 2011. "Gender and Finance in Sub-Saharan Africa: Are Women Disadvantaged?" Policy Research Working Paper 5571, World Bank, Washington, DC.

Autio, E. 2007. *The 2007 Global Entrepreneurship Monitor Special Topic Report: High-Growth Entrepreneurship,* www.gemconsortium.org.

————. 2008. "High-and-Low Aspiration Entrepreneurship and Economic Growth in Low-Income Economies." Paper presented at the UNU-WIDER

Workshop on Entrepreneurship in Economic Development, Helsinki, Finland, August 21–23.

Baumol, W. J. 1990. "Entrepreneurship: Productive, Unproductive and Destructive." *Journal of Political Economy* 98 (5): 893–921.

Boserup, E. 1970. *Woman's Role in Economic Development*. London: Earthscan.

Chamlee-Wright, E. 1997. *The Cultural Foundations Economic Development*. London and New York: Routledge.

Devine, T. J. 1994a. "Changes in Wage-and-Salary Returns to Skill and the Recent Rise in Female Self-Employment." *American Economic Review* 84 (2): 108–12.

———. 1994b. "Characteristics of Self-Employed Women in the United States." *Monthly Labor Review* 117 (3): 20–34.

Evans, D., and B. Jovanovic. 1989. "An Estimated Model of Entrepreneurial Choice under Liquidity Constraints." *Journal of Political Economy* 97 (4): 808–27.

Georgellis, Y., and H. Wall. 2005. "Gender Differences in Self-Employment." *International Review of Applied Economics* 19 (3): 321–37.

Ghani, E., W. R. Kerr, and S. O'Connell. 2011. "Promoting Entrepreneurship, Growth, and Job Creation." In *Reshaping Tomorrow* ed. Ejaz Ghani. New York: Oxford University Press.

Goedhuys, M., and L. Sleuwaegen. 2010. "High Growth Entrepreneurial Firms in Africa: A Quantile Regression Approach." *Small Business Economics* 34 (1): 31–51.

Gries, T., and W. A. Naudé. 2009. "Entrepreneurship and Regional Economic Growth: Towards a General Theory of Start-Ups." *Innovation: The European Journal of Social Science Research* 22 (3): 309–28.

———. 2010. "Entrepreneurship and Structural Economic Transformation." *Small Business Economics Journal* 34 (1): 13–29.

GTZ, World Bank, and Inter-American Development Bank (IDB). 2010. *Women's Economic Opportunities in the Formal Private Sector in Latin America and the Caribbean: A Focus on Entrepreneurship*. Washington, DC: World Bank.

ILO (International Labour Organization). 2005a. *Support for Growth Oriented Women Entrepreneurs in Ethiopia*. Geneva: ILO.

———. 2005b. *Support for Growth Oriented Women Entrepreneurs in Kenya*. Geneva: ILO.

———. 2005c. *Support for Growth Oriented Women Entrepreneurs in Tanzania*. Geneva: ILO.

Kelley, D., N. Bosma, and J. E. Amorós. 2011. *The 2010 Global Entrepreneurship Monitor Global Report*. Babson Park, MA: Center for Women's Leadership, Babson College, http://www.gemconsortium.org.

Kim, G. 2007. "The Analysis of Self-Employment Levels over the Life-Cycle." *Quarterly Review of Economics and Finance* 47 (3): 397–410.

Kirzner, I. M. 1973. *Competition and Entrepreneurship.* Chicago: University of Chicago Press.

Klapper, L., and I. Love. 2010. "The Impact of the Financial Crisis on New Firm Registration." Policy Research Working Paper 5444, World Bank, Washington, DC.

Krueger, A. 1974. "The Political Economy of the Rent Seeking Society." *American Economic Review* 64 (3): 291–303.

Leff, N. 1979. "Entrepreneurship and Economic Development: The Problem Revisited." *Journal of Economic Literature* 17 (1): 46–64.

Lewis, W. A. 1954. "Economic Development with Unlimited Supplies of Labour." *Manchester School* 28 (2): 139–91.

Minniti, M. 2009. "Gender Issues in Entrepreneurship." *Foundations and Trends in Entrepreneurship* 5 (7/8): 497–621.

———. 2010. "Female Entrepreneurship and Economic Activity." *European Journal of Development Research* 22 (3): 294–312.

Minniti, M., and C. Nardone. 2007. "Being in Someone Else's Shoes: Gender and Nascent Entrepreneurship." *Small Business Economics* 28 (2): 223–39.

Minniti, M., and W. A. Naudé. 2010. "What Do We Know about the Patterns and Determinants of Female Entrepreneurship across Countries?" *European Journal of Development Research* 22 (2): 1–17.

Nallari, R., and B. Griffith. 2011. *Gender and Macroeconomic Policy.* Washington, DC: World Bank.

Naudé, W. A. 2007. "Peace, Prosperity and Pro-Growth Entrepreneurship." UNU-WIDER Discussion Paper WDP 2007/02, United Nations University, Helsinki, Finland.

———. 2008. "Entrepreneurship in Economic Development." UNU-WIDER Research Paper 2008/20, United Nations University, Helsinki, Finland.

———. 2009. "Entrepreneurship, Post-Conflict." In *Making Peace Work: The Challenges of Social and Economic Reconstruction,* ed. T. Addison and T. Brück, 251–63. Basingstoke: Palgrave Macmillan.

———. 2010a. "Entrepreneurship, Developing Countries and Development Economics: New Approaches and Insights." *Small Business Economics Journal* 34 (1): 1–12.

———. 2010b. "Promoting Entrepreneurship in Developing Countries: Policy Challenges." UNU Policy Brief 4, United Nations University, Tokyo.

———. 2010c. "Entrepreneurship, Global Development, and the Policy Challenge." *Harvard College Economic Review* 4 (2): 24–25.

Naudé, W. A., T. Gries, E. Wood, and A. Meintjes. 2008. "Regional Determinants of Entrepreneurial Start-Ups in a Developing Country." *Entrepreneurship and Regional Development* 20 (2): 111–24.

Nyström, K. 2008. "Is Entrepreneurship the Salvation for Enhanced Economic Growth?" Electronic Working Papers 143, Center of Excellence for Science and Innovation Studies, Royal Institute of Technology, Sweden.

OECD (Organisation for Economic Co-operation and Development). 1998. *Women Entrepreneurs in Small and Medium Enterprises.* Paris: OECD.

Schumpeter, J. A. 1942. *Capitalism, Socialism and Democracy.* New York: New York.

———. 1961. *The Theory of Economic Development.* New York: University Press.

Stiglitz, J. 2006. "Civil Strife and Economic and Social Policies." *Economics of Peace and Security Journal* 1 (1): 6–9.

Terjesen, S., and J. E. Amorós. 2010. "Female Entrepreneurship in Latin America and the Caribbean: Characteristics, Drivers and Relationship to Economic Development." *European Journal of Development Research* 22 (3): 313–30.

Thurik, Roy, and Ingrid Verheul. 2001. "Start-Up Capital: "Does Gender Matter?" *Small Business Economics* 16 (4): 329–45.

Ucbasaran, D., G. A. Alsos, P. Westhead, and M. Wright. 2008. "Habitual Entrepreneurs." *Foundations and Trends in Entrepreneurship* 4 (4): 309–450.

Valenzuela, María Elena. 2004. "Microempresa en América Latina: Nuevas Oportunidades o Callejón Sin Salida para las Mujeres?" [Microenterprises in Latin America: New Opportunities or a Dead End for Women?]. In *Nuevo Sendero para las Mujeres? Microempresa y Género en América Latina en el Umbral del Siglo XXI* [A New Path for Women? Microenterprise and Gender in Latin America on the Cusp of the XXI Century], ed. María Elena Valenzuela, 19–72. Santiago de Chile: Centro de Estudios de la Mujer [Center for Women's Studies].

Wong, P. K., Y. P. Ho, and E. Autio. 2005. "Entrepreneurship, Innovation and Economic Growth: Evidence from GEM Data." *Small Business Economics* 24 (3): 335–50.

World Bank. 2003. *Brazil: Inequality and Economic Development.* Washington, DC: World Bank.

———. 2005a. *Peru: Opportunities for All: Peru Poverty Assessment.* Washington, DC: World Bank.

———. 2005b. *Bolivia: Poverty Assessment.* Washington, DC: World Bank.

———. 2005c. *Country Assistance Strategy for the Oriental Republic of Uruguay, 2005–2010.* Washington, DC: World Bank.

————. 2007. *Evaluating Mexico's Small and Medium Enterprise Programs.* Washington, DC: World Bank.

————. 2010. *Women's Economic Opportunities in the Formal Private Sector in Latin America and the Caribbean: A Focus on Entrepreneurship.* Washington, DC: World Bank.

World Economic Forum (WEF). 2004. *Global Competitiveness Report,* http://www.weforum.org.

Yunus, M. 2007. "The Nobel Peace Prize 2006: Nobel Lecture." *Law and Business Review of the Americas* 13 (2): 267–75.

CHAPTER 6

Globalization and Jobs

What first comes to mind when thinking about globalization is the tremendous growth in cross-border trade flows. This growth has occurred not just in merchandise trade but also in trade in services: the value of trade (goods and services) as a percentage of world gross domestic product (GDP) increased from 42 percent in 1980 to 62 percent in 2007. Broadly speaking, however, economic globalization refers to the greater integration of national economies into the international economy, not only through trade but also through foreign direct investment, capital flows, migration, and the spread of technology. This integration has gradually taken place over time, but its pace has accelerated over recent decades. According to the International Monetary Fund, foreign direct investment increased from 6.5 percent of world GDP in 1980 to 31.8 percent in 2006; the stock of international claims (primarily bank loans) as a percentage of world GDP increased from roughly 10 percent in 1980 to 48 percent in 2006; and the number of minutes spent on cross-border telephone calls, on a per capita basis, increased from 7.3 in 1991 to 28.8 in 2006 (IMF 2008).

The integration of the global marketplace is believed to generate significant opportunities for both producers and consumers to take advantage of the larger and more diversified markets around the world, leading to better access to cheaper imports (as well as technology) and larger export markets. It is also thought to enhance efficiency through specialization and competition. While an integrated and open trading system is generally associated with economic growth and prosperity, questions—often concerns—have been raised about the implications for various groups' in society. Would the benefits of increased efficiency or larger markets be shared by all? In particular, the potential impact of globalization on workers' employment and wages has led to heated debates and even to some violent backlash. This section discusses some of the key aspects of the relationships between globalization and jobs—an important issue for policy makers and politicians in many countries.

Correlation or Causality?

At the outset, it should be noted that economic integration or globalization can be driven by a large variety of factors. It could reflect the outcomes of policy decisions, such as the removal of trade or regulatory barriers. Indeed, recent decades have been characterized by significant trade liberalization at the multilateral level (for example, the Uruguay Round), at the regional level (through the proliferation of regional trading arrangements), and especially at the national level (through unilateral reforms). At the same time, a lot of non-policy-related developments have greatly facilitated the process of global integration. These were mainly driven by exogenous progress in science and technology. The most vivid illustration is the revolution in the information and communication technologies (ICT) that allowed cheaper, faster, easier interactions among economic agents from different corners of the globe. Technological progress also led to important declines in shipping costs and shipping times. Hence, not all observed interaction between globalization and jobs should be attributed to changes in trade policy.

It is also very important to keep in mind that the same exogenous factors (for example, technological progress like computerization) that affect trade flows (due to more efficient shipping or communication technologies) could directly affect the demand for workers, as they are replaced by new computers or machines. Thus, one needs to be very careful in inferring a causal relationship from an observed correlation between trade integration and labor market outcomes. The fact that there is a correlation between trade and wages, for instance, does not necessarily imply that trade affects wages. This correlation has been one of the main challenges facing researchers investigating the topic.

Wages or Employment

The effects of globalization on the labor market can be observed mainly through changes in the wage rates, in employment, or in both. The exact nature and composition of the impact varies from country to country and depends on the existing policy environment, including labor market institutions and rigidities or social policies. When wages are flexibly set in decentralized labor markets (for example, in the United Kingdom and the United States), a decline in relative demand for labor would translate into lower relative wages. In contrast, when wages are rigid and set in centralized labor markets (for example, in France, Germany, and Italy), it would mean lower relative employment.[1]

In many developing countries, wage responses seem to be greater than employment impact, and evidence suggests that trade liberalization leads to significant declines in the wage premiums in those sectors that experienced the largest tariff reductions. This finding can be explained by the prevalence of labor market distortions and related rigidities that prevent labor reallocation in the short to medium term or by the dissipation of industry rents that have been supported by the trade policy stance (Hoekman and Winters 2007). The latter is enhanced by an imperfect output market: many firms adjusted to trade reform by reducing profit margins (adjusting wages) and raising productivity rather than by laying off workers.[2] In a study of Mexico's trade liberalization, Revenga (1997) finds that workers have appropriated some of the rents from protection in a way that the procompetitive effects of trade reduced not only profits but also wages in the manufacturing sector.

Potential Links between Openness and the Labor Market

Different channels exist through which greater economic integration can affect jobs and workers in a particular country. Conceptually, international trade can influence the prices of goods and services in both exporting and importing countries. Changes in product prices brought about by trade alter the profit opportunities facing firms, inciting them to shift resources away from industries in which profitability has fallen and toward those where it has risen. This shift, in turn, affects the returns to labor (that is, the wage rates) by altering the demand for workers.[3] The following points suggest the ways in which globalization affects the wage rate and employment:

- Increased imports put pressures on import-competing industries and can drive down prices and provide incentives for restructuring. This restructuring, in turn, can lead to a decline in the demand for labor and employment opportunities (and a decrease in the wage paid to workers) in those industries.[4]

- To the extent that workers are themselves consumers of imported goods, the downward pressure on prices induced by increased imports will (other things being equal) tend to improve their welfare by increasing their real wages. Similarly, the worker-consumer will gain from a more diversified bundle of goods.

- Increased imports of intermediate goods or raw materials would raise the profitability and competitiveness of firms that use them to sell either in the domestic market or in the export markets. Under normal circumstances, this increase will lead to a greater demand for labor, associated with higher wages, by those firms.

- To the extent that technology can complement workers (that is, by enhancing their productivity), import of technology-embodied goods can lead to higher demand (and higher wages) for the type of (skilled) workers that can take advantage of the new technology (Acemoglu 2003). However, if technology (say, mechanization) tends to substitute for a given type of (unskilled) workers, increased import of technological goods will tend to decrease the demand and wages for those workers.

- The vent-for-surplus thesis suggests that trade provides access to a large global market and thus allows an economy to productively employ reservoirs of surplus labor. By increasing product prices, increased exports can enhance the profitability of firms in exporting industries and can lead to an expansion of employment opportunities as well as the wage rate in those industries.

- Another important feature of the current wave of globalization is the increased flow of capital. Capital flows that effectively change a country's stock of capital (relative to labor) can affect the relative price of labor[5] in both the source and the recipient countries. For the recipient country, to the extent that more capital can make a given number of workers more productive, an inflow of capital would likely increase input per worker and tend to increase the wage rate.[6] In general, inflow of new capital requires hiring new workers; however, in some cases where labor and capital are relatively substitutable, capital could make labor so productive that fewer workers would be demanded. For the source countries, the claim is often made that outflows of capital can lower wages as multinational firms establish (or expand) overseas affiliates and then "export" or outsource jobs.

Short- versus Long-Run Impacts

Standard theoretical trade models, with their "full-employment" assumption, predict that trade and trade policy changes will affect sectoral employment and wage rates but will not have an impact on the overall level of employment. Empirical cross-country and country-specific evidence, however, seems to suggest a potentially adverse impact in the short run followed by a positive (albeit small) effect on aggregate employment in the long run following greater trade integration (Hoekman and Winters 2007). Rama (2003) finds a negative short-run impact of trade on wages (a 20-percentage-point increase in the trade-to-GDP ratio leads to a 5 percent drop in wages), which becomes positive after four years and strongly positive after five.

For policy makers, short-run political considerations might be more important as they are more likely to influence voter sentiments. In the short run, workers are not really mobile across sectors since human capital tends to be sector specific. Thus, trade opening would tend to increase unemployment as it destroys jobs in the liberalizing sectors, with limited adjustments in the other sectors of the economy not directly affected by the shock. It may take time for displaced workers to find new jobs in other sectors. The adjustment can occur only in the medium to long run, when labor has time to move across sectors, from inefficient import-competing sectors to exporting sectors or sectors in which the country has a comparative advantage.

Of course, the effects on a particular country would ultimately depend on what "greater trade integration" actually entails. If the labor content of imports and exports does not dramatically change, one could intuitively posit that a variation in a country's trade balance would affect the aggregate employment in the same direction: an increase in the trade deficit would tend to be associated with an increase in employment and vice versa. Long-run employment gains can result when accessing international markets permits expansion and accumulation in successful sectors and as the (second-order) benefits of trade openness start to kick in and generate more economic activity. Whatever the direction, the magnitude of the effects of greater trade integration on overall wages and aggregate employment is found to be small (Hoekman and Winters 2007). However, trade can at best be considered a minor determinant of the long-run levels of employment and unemployment.[7]

Are Adjustments Intersectoral or Intrasectoral?

The impact of globalization on the labor market can manifest itself at the aggregate national level, at the intersectoral level, and at the intrasectoral level. As was discussed in the previous section, the effects at the sectoral level tend to be more significant than economywide aggregate ones. At the sectoral level, an important distinction is made between intersectoral and intrasectoral adjustment.

While there is some evidence of a relatively weak negative impact of import competition on sectoral employment, recent literature finds that trade liberalization has far smaller effects on cross-sectoral labor shifts than is often presumed and that the bulk of the impact tends to be concentrated at the intrasectoral level (see, for example, Wacziarg and Wallak 2004). Despite the extensive trade liberalization in many Latin American countries during the 1980s and 1990s, no evidence of large-scale reallocation of workers across sectors has been found. Instead, for a set of Latin American countries trade liberalization appears to have increased the pace of within-industry job reallocation, as inefficient incumbent firms were displaced by more efficient entrants. Similarly, there was more intrasectoral than intersectoral labor mobility as a result of trade liberalization in the United Kingdom's manufacturing sector during the period 1995–2000.

Recent studies using firm-level data conclude that the major impacts of trade reforms are the natural selection among firms and reductions in x-inefficiency: more efficient firms within a sector expand their market shares, while less efficient firms in a sector are forced to exit, downsize, or improve their efficiency (Melitz 2003). For instance, using plant-level Chilean data for 1976–86, Levinsohn (1999) found that while macroeconomic shocks and trade liberalization lowered manufacturing employment by 8 percent, nearly 25 percent of all workers switched jobs, with larger firms expanding at the expense of smaller ones. As a result, overall total factor productivity increased (and potentially wages rose as well) in industries that liberalized more. However, it should be noted that in this case, job destruction could outweigh job creation within a given industry—not all displaced workers are absorbed by the more productive firms that increase their market share.

Just as imports can eliminate less efficient firms, exports can encourage more efficient firms to expand. Firm-level analyses also find that within a given sector, exporters tend to be more productive than other plants[8] and tend to pay higher wages (Bernard, Jensen, and Lawrence 1995; OECD 2010b). This finding seems to be valid for firms broadly involved in international trade (exporters or importers of inputs or intermediaries). A recent paper based on Enterprise Surveys data from the Europe and Central Asia region and from Latin America and the Caribbean finds that firms that both import and export are almost four times as large, are twice as productive, and pay six times more wages than nontrading firms (Seker 2009).[9] Van Biesebroeck (2005) reports that, in a number of African countries, exporting firms pay, on average, 34 percent higher wages.

Similarly, globally engaged firms (those with foreign ownership) create more jobs, pay higher wages, and are more productive than firms that are purely domestically owned. Higher foreign investment in a particular industry is usually associated with higher wages in that industry because of the transfer of technology by multinational firms from the parent to its affiliates. Interestingly, however, little evidence seems to indicate that the newly transferred technology spills over to the rest of the economy to increase the productivity and wages of workers in domestically owned firms. In a study of Mexico and República Bolivariana de Venezuela, Aitken, Harrison, and Lipsey (1996) find that foreign direct investment raises wages only within the plants of the foreign affiliates, not in the rest of the economy.

Has Globalization Led to Increased Inequality?

The standard model of international trade makes clear and elegant predictions about the patterns of trade and their impact on the various factors of production. In the model, rich economies specialize in the production of commodities that require relatively high levels of skill and trade those for goods from developing countries whose production requires relatively little skilled labor. According to the model, while these are beneficial exchanges, they generate winners and losers: high-skilled workers in rich countries gain, while their low-skilled peers lose, tending to increase inequality in those countries. In developing countries, low-skilled workers gain, while their high-skilled colleagues lose. While these predictions are very stylized and depend on some restrictive assumptions, they have sparked heated debates about the potential (distributive) impact of the current wave of globalization.

The main concern about globalization relates to the growing evidence of a significant increase in the relative reward for skilled labor—the so-called skills premium. This premium has been accompanied by a steady shift in demand away from the less skilled toward the more skilled in all sectors. What differs from the theoretical prediction is that this rising inequality between skilled and unskilled workers has occurred not only in rich economies but also in developing countries.

A large literature investigates whether this growing skill premium is the result of globalization or instead is caused by other exogenous factors—particularly technological progress, as suggested earlier.[10] While the debate is still continuing, available evidence points to the fact that trade flows and trade policy reforms can explain only a small fraction (about 20 percent) of the observed general increase in wage inequality in both developed and developing economies (WTO 2008). Theory suggests that if import competition has contributed to the rising income equality, one should be able to observe a decline in the price of products made by low-skilled labor relative to the price of products made by skilled labor (which, in turn, would induce domestic firms to shift toward producing skill-intensive goods). In reality, little evidence of large relative price increases in skilled-labor-intensive goods has been found.

The rapid technological progress that has enhanced the productivity of skilled workers (and decreased the need for unskilled ones)—the so-called skill-biased technical change—appears to be the main culprit.[11] That is, the increased prevalence of computers and other technologies in both rich and poor economies has raised the productivity and wages of workers with high levels of human capital, while having little impact on the wages of less-skilled workers. Acemoglu (2003) contends that trade may still be a driver as imports of high-tech intermediate inputs could have raised the productivity of skilled labor. Feenstra and Hanson (2003) argue that a simultaneous rise in wage inequality in both developed and developing countries can occur when tasks that are intensive in medium skills (that is, considered low skills in rich countries but high skills in poor countries) are moved—or outsourced—from developed countries to developing countries, leading to a rise in average skill intensity everywhere (see more below).

The increase in the relative demand for skilled labor in developing countries is also found to be positively correlated with the change in the number of foreign-affiliate assembly plants. Some evidence shows that, like technological advances, foreign direct investment increases the wages of skilled workers relative to unskilled labor. A possible explanation is that the techniques used by foreign investors, while less skill intensive in the context of their home country endowments, are relatively skill intensive in the context of the host country (Feenstra 2007). Feenstra and Hanson (1996), for instance, study the case in which U.S. multinationals outsource intermediate input production to Mexican *maquiladora* plants; they find that the production of this input is relatively unskilled labor intensive from the U.S. perspective but skill intensive from the Mexican perspective. As a result, the relatively skilled workers' wage rate is pushed up in both Mexico and the United States.

Evolving Nature of Globalization: Offshoring

Recent analyses have argued that the failure to find a strong relationship between trade and wages may not necessarily reflect a limited influence of trade on labor market outcomes but rather a failure to account for the new dimensions of the globalized economy. Krugman (2008) and Feenstra (2008), for instance, point to an outdated conception of the workings of the global economy. For a long time, most international trade meant the exchange of "finished goods": that is, most of the tasks required to manufacture a given product were undertaken within a single country. With the recent improvements in transportation and communication technology, however, a new pattern of trade has emerged in which different countries perform specific tasks and add value to global supply chains.

Shifting jobs or shipping specific tasks to lower-wage countries is an increasingly popular practice among businesses seeking to cut operating costs. It can increase productivity, enhance company competitiveness, and improve the bottom line. Yi (2003) estimates that half the rapid growth in merchandise trade between 1962 and 1999 can be accounted for by national specialization in specific tasks in the manufacturing supply chain. Similarly, Feenstra and Hanson (1996) find that after 1972, the volume of imported intermediate goods used in production of U.S. manufactures rose substantially. This increase has not been confined to merchandise trade: it has also grown significantly in the context of trade in services. This phenomenon—variously described as trade in intermediates and tasks, fragmentation, offshoring, outsourcing, slicing up the value chain, or vertical specialization—affects the demand for different types of workers and has important implications for global labor markets. To date, little evidence points to any significant (positive or adverse) effects of offshoring on overall employment—either in absolute terms or in relative terms (that is, relative to the effects of import penetration) (OECD 2010b).

Not surprisingly, this new trend has triggered concerns that certain kinds of tasks or jobs in developed countries will be "exported" or "outsourced" to developing countries where workers are paid less, are equally skilled in a wide range of tasks, and are willing to perform the more mundane chores that workers in rich countries are less inclined to do. While decreasing production costs, this "trade in tasks" generates effects that could be biased against a particular subset of the labor force—those whose tasks are most likely to be offshored. Within a particular country, labor will be reallocated toward certain kinds of tasks and away from others.

Any task not requiring direct interaction with the local marketplace or immediate physical delivery can technically be outsourced. Indeed, Blinder (2006) argues that almost 40 million American jobs are at risk of being offshored over the next 20 years, and he suggests that American workers better specialize in personal services.[12] But which tasks are the most vulnerable? The current wisdom suggests that routine, codifiable tasks that can be conducted through stable and predictable processes are most likely to be either mechanized or shipped to lower-cost countries. Tasks requiring nonroutine interpersonal interactions or complex problem-solving skills tend to be placebound. As a consequence of either task-biased technological change (routine tasks are being mechanized) or international trade (routine tasks are outsourced to developing countries), the economic or business structure of rich countries has gradually shifted from an emphasis on routine to nonroutine tasks (even at the firm level). It has been shown that the ratio of nonroutine to routine workers increases with trade with developing economies and that workers performing nonroutine tasks find their wages less strongly affected by trade with developing economies than workers who perform routine tasks (see, for example, Autor 2003). Related to the debate on wage inequality discussed earlier, Feenstra and Hanson (1996) find that while technical change (in the form of capital expenditures) is responsible for the lion's share of the wage premium enjoyed by skilled workers, outsourcing remains a major and significant driver of the wage differential.

Factor Mobility: Migration

Another key feature of globalization is the movement of workers from one country to another. Evidently, such movements will affect wages and employment in both source and destination countries. Because immigration is more visible (even more intrusive), however, it tends to be met with more political and social resistance than trade. Consequently, cross-border flows of workers have grown relatively slower than flows of goods or capital.[13] In recent decades as globalization has accelerated, the flow of goods and services (trade) and capital (finance) across boundaries has increased enormously. However, labor movement across countries, particularly from poorer to richer nations, has not been commensurate with the rapid pace of trade and capital flows: the number of foreign workers increased from 78 million people (2.4 percent of world population) in 1965 to 191 million people (3.0 percent of world population) in 2005.

In many respects, immigration is similar to imports as well as to outsourcing. Both can lead to economic efficiency and potentially be beneficial, but they both produce winners and losers. Both are driven (at least partially) by an incentive to take advantage of the relatively high wages in the destination economy. In the case of immigration, the workers themselves move, whereas in the case of imports, it is the services of the lower-wage workers that are shipped. Either way, the "effective" supply of workers in the destination will expand. This factor, in turn, will tend to depress wages and reduce employment opportunities for native workers. It should be noted that while the bulk of the attention is on the potential impact of the unskilled workers from poor countries who move to more advanced countries, immigration could also entail the movement of skilled workers—that is, scientists and engineers with significant human capital. Such immigration can potentially lead to increased investment and to higher wages and growth rates in the destination countries.

From the perspective of the source country, the outflow of workers can increase the wage rate since it leads to a relative scarcity. The migration of skilled workers could also lead to a brain drain, depriving the country of much-needed human capital and potentially reducing the productivity of the remaining (unskilled) workers. At the same time, migration generates a flow of capital from the destination to the source country in the form of remittances, which some argue account for most of the benefits of migration for developing countries. A recent World Bank study (2006) has estimated that if the rich countries allowed just a 3 percent rise in their labor force through relaxing restrictions on immigration, the likely annual benefit would be US$300 billion to the poorer countries (about four times the current aid transfers of US$70 billion per year) and US$51 billion to the richer countries.

Impact of the 2008 Financial Crisis on Employment

For several decades, developing countries have complemented external official sources of funding with private forms of financing to support their development. As increasing globalization led to the removal of barriers to resource flows, cross-border movements of private capital have become an important feature of the global economy and dominate capital flows for many developing countries, especially for emerging markets. But these capital flows have been volatile, with large swings, as when capital flows sharply increased before the East Asian and other financial crises in emerging markets in the mid-1990s, followed by abrupt declines at the onset of the crises.

In the years preceding the recent global financial crisis, the flow of private capital again surged into developing countries. Between 2005 and 2007, net private capital flows to these countries rose to unprecedented levels, peaking at US$1.2 trillion in 2007 (see table 6.1). Strong performance in emerging economies and relatively higher rates of return in these economies were partly responsible. As the global financial crisis unfolded, however, many emerging markets experienced substantial capital outflows combined with sharply reduced inflows. It became more difficult and more expensive to access international capital markets as investors became strongly risk averse and sought safe havens in Europe and the United States.

Table 6.1   Net International Capital Flows to Developing Countries, 2005–10[b]
(US$ millions)

	2005	2006	2007	2008	2009[a]	2010[b]
Net private inflows	573.3	732.1	1,223.7	752.4	454.0	589.5
Net equity inflows	349.9	469.0	663.8	536.5	445.9	497.5
Net debt flows	223.4	263.1	559.9	215.9	8.1	92.0

Source: World Bank 2010.
a. Estimated.
b. Forecast.

As a result, net private capital flows to developing countries in 2008 were US$752 billion, compared to the US$1.2 trillion recorded just a year earlier (table 6.1).[14] For 2010, projections indicate that net private flows will be around US$590 billion, 30 percent higher than the 2009 estimates. However, this is still much lower than the peak level of 2007. As capital flows begin to recover somewhat, low interest rates in advanced countries are making some emerging markets attractive destinations for international investors for (short-term) investments. Some countries are receiving large capital inflows and having to resort to various measures to mitigate the adverse macroeconomic impacts.

Global GDP growth as well as GDP growth in all regions was lower in 2009 than in 2007. More specifically, negative growth rates were observed during 2009 in developed countries, the European Union (EU), Central and southeastern Europe, countries in the Commonwealth of Independent States (CIS), and, to a lesser extent, Latin America and the Caribbean. Growth rates in 2009 were positive, though, in East Asia, South Asia, the Middle East, North Africa, and Sub-Saharan Africa, although lower than in 2007.

Along with the slower growth, all regions experienced higher unemployment, with the highest being in the developed economies, the EU, Central and southeastern Europe, CIS, and Latin America and the Caribbean, which again all had negative GDP growth rates in 2009 (see table 6.2). The International Labour Organization (ILO) estimates that the global crisis has led to 34 million more unemployed, and the World Bank estimates that about 60 million people may have been pushed into poverty.

Table 6.2   Change in Output and Unemployment between 2007 and 2009
(percent)

	Change in real GDP growth rate	Change in unemployment rate
World	−6.3	0.9
Developed economies and EU	−6.1	2.7
Central and southeastern Europe and CIS	−14.1	2.0
East Asia	5.1	0.6
South Asia	−3.7	0.1
Latin America and the Caribbean	−8.2	1.2
Middle East	−4.7	0.1
North Africa	−2.1	0.4
Sub-Saharan Africa	−5.6	0.2

Source: Authors' computations based on data from ILO 2010.

Women have been more severely affected in countries where gender differences in unemployment were high to begin with. Youth unemployment has also shown an upward tick since the crisis and is currently at an all-time high. According to the ILO, 81 million out of 630 million 15–24-year-olds were unemployed at the end of 2009. This number is 7.8 million more than at the end of 2007. The largest reductions both in employment and in working hours were observed in manufacturing (export-oriented industries, including the garments and textiles, electronics, iron and steel, and automobile sectors) and in construction in most of the countries. Estimates of underemployment are sketchy but add to the problem. In addition, the global downturn has displaced quite a lot of migrant workers.

Striving for decent work has become the main priority in a number of regions of the world. Fiscal stimulus packages in more than 40 countries were aimed at supporting a global recovery. On average, about 1.4 percent of world GDP was to be allotted for fiscal stimulus packages during 2009–10, with the United States (5.6 percent of its GDP), China (13 percent of its GDP), Saudi Arabia, and Malaysia being among the largest; for OECD countries, fiscal stimulus averaged 3.5 percent of 2008 GDP. The aggregate fiscal stimulus for the G-20 (Group of 20) countries, which includes discretionary and nondiscretionary automatic stabilizers, was estimated to be 2.6 percent of GDP for 2009.

The measures undertaken by countries in response to the jobs crisis can be broadly grouped into four areas: (a) stimulating employment generation; (b) providing social protection through income support to workers and families; (c) implementing labor market policies to support job seekers and the unemployed; and (d) promoting social dialogue and consultations with business and labor on measures to counter the crisis. In a 2009 ILO survey that covered 54 countries, it was found that all countries gave high priority to new or additional investments in infrastructure with the aim of generating employment. Middle- and lower-income countries typically invested more heavily in the expansion of social protection, while the high-income countries focused more on labor market policies for the unemployed.

The ILO estimates that 7–11 million jobs were created or saved in the G-20 countries in 2009 by stimulus packages. The jobs created or saved were equivalent to 29–43 percent of the total increase in unemployment of 25 million in G-20 countries for the first half of 2009. Without such spending, unemployment would probably have been much higher in these countries. That being said, in view of the current output and employment figures, the overall impact of the fiscal packages on output and employment thus far can be said to be mixed at best. Even though trade volumes have recovered quickly, for various reasons the pace of economic recovery has been slow: the smaller magnitude of fiscal multipliers, long delays between legislation and spending, bad design of the packages (for example, the U.S. stimulus was spent not on construction or infrastructure but on public servants' salaries, health care, school teachers, police, and alternative energy sources, all of which are important for society but do not create many new jobs).[15]

In the United States, small and medium firms (fewer than 500 employees) have generated most of the jobs in the recent past. However, recent research (for example, Haltiwanger, Scarpetta, and Schweiger 2010) indicates that it is start-up and younger businesses that contribute to gross and net job creation; the size of the firm does not necessarily matter for job creation. The fiscal stimulus packages did not provide many benefits to this segment or reduce the uncertainty about starting up new businesses. In addition, in the United States as well as in Europe labor mobility has decreased, in part because those workers with sizable home mortgages are unable to sell their houses and relocate as the housing market has crashed. Worker mobility also appears to be constrained by rapid urbanization, which has resulted in exorbitant urban housing prices and rents.

In addition, the current higher unemployment rates observed in the United States and in other developed economies may be a phenomenon that fiscal spending may not be able to eradicate easily. In these countries, there appears to be a longer trend toward structural unemployment, with the hiring being lower than the job openings because of mismatched skills. More broadly, empirical data show that employment for workers with medium skills in the advanced countries has been falling since 2000. Many economists believe that the advanced economies are undergoing structural change whereby medium-skilled jobs are being replaced with cheaper technology and automation or are being offshored and outsourced to China, India, and elsewhere. The recent economic crisis could have given the ongoing structural change a boost: medium-skilled workers laid off during the crisis may not be replaced even if the economy picks up again. For example, managers may have gotten used to answering their phones and managing their calendars with the help of an iPhone or Blackberry. If this is the case, the economic crisis would have medium-term and even long-term effects by significantly increasing the number of long-term unemployed and consequently the number of people who withdraw from the labor force.

Under such circumstances, to have a substantial impact on the unemployment rate, fiscal spending would need to include massive but effective relevant training and retraining programs to retool the unemployed with market-relevant skills.

For developing countries, the economic crisis has sent shocks through large declines in exports, capital inflows, and remittances, all of which tend to affect both employment and wages. Fewer exports lead to the loss of modern-sectors jobs, which typically pay better than those in the informal economy. Decreases in capital inflows lead to slower growth in employment. Therefore, declines in both exports and capital inflows not only raise unemployment in the formal sector but also increase the number of workers in the already crowded informal sector, further increasing underemployment and lowering productivity and consequently increasing the numbers of the working poor. Declines in remittances will have negative short- and longer-term effects on recipient households, because, apart from being a significant source of income, remittances from migrants are also an important source of finance for education. Children of remittance-recipient households in El Salvador and Sri Lanka, for example, have been found to have lower dropout rates and are more likely to receive private education. Therefore, declines in remittances will negatively affect the skills acquisition of the workers of the next generation.

In summary, there are good grounds for concerns that fiscal stimuli (and monetary easing) will not be able to prevent the economic crisis from having long-term negative effects on the global as well as on the national labor markets for both advanced and developing countries. Some worry that the longer-term trend will be one of jobless economic growth, particularly in the developed economies. Others worry that the future of industrialization is one of joblessness; and while the service sector will still generate jobs, technological innovation is higher in industry than in services. The job crisis has been and will continue to be complex and subject to many influences. Beyond sound fiscal and monetary policies, what are needed are structural reforms in trade in goods and services as well as in manufacturing and agro-processing for low-income countries; a higher quality of education, including through use of ICT; more relevant skills training; and a host of labor market policies.

Notes

1. It has been argued that rigidities in European labor markets limit the speed of adjustment to import competition, so that adverse effects tend to last longer than in the United States.

2. When there is substantial rent sharing between protected firms and their workers, trade liberalization erodes these rents, with the incidence of the loss shared between the two factors and the precise shares depending on country-specific variables. This may also be related to the relative bargaining power of the different factors sharing the rents.

3. Alternatively, trade can be viewed as effectively shipping from one country to another the services of the workers engaged in the production of traded goods. All else equal, imports add to the labor endowment (thus reducing the wage rates) of the importing country and reduce the effective stock of labor (thus raising wages) in the exporting country.

4. It should be noted that import competition could motivate firms to shift their workers to the informal sector where there are fewer "constraints," such as minimum wages, hiring and firing regulations, or benefits.

5. Cross-border capital flows have increased rapidly since the 1970s, growing at a rate much higher than that of trade in goods.

6. Rama (2003) finds that a one-percentage-point increase in the ratio of foreign direct investment to GDP is associated with a 1 percent wage increase.

7. In a study using data for a large number of developing countries, McMillan and Verduzco (2010) report that over the period 1980–2006, there has been minimal correlation between trade and aggregate industrial employment. A similar result is found in OECD (2007).

8. Perhaps because exporting tends to be more skill intensive (Harrison and Hanson 1999).

9. This naturally raises the question whether this is self-selection (productive firms are better able to export), or whether it is the decision to target the export markets that makes firms more productive.

10. Scholars have addressed this question through two approaches. One seeks to delineate the factors of production embodied in trade flows. The second examines the extent to which trade induces changes in the relative prices of goods that are intensive in skilled and unskilled workers and ultimately in the relative wages. Overall, there is no evidence that trade is a significant factor driving earnings inequality in developed economies.

11. Brown (2010) nicely summarizes the potential explanations on why globalization cannot be the main driver of the growing inequality. First, the volume of trade has not been large enough or sufficiently intensive in unskilled labor. Second, prices of unskilled-labor-intensive imports were not falling. And third, virtually all industries shifted away from unskilled-labor-intensive production techniques even as unskilled labor became cheaper. See also Goldberg and Pavcnik (2005).

12. Jensen and Kletzer (2008) counter that the number of "at risk" jobs is much lower, 15–20 million, and that any job losses will be offset by job gains in services exports (and "inshoring"). They also document that while the jobs

that are likely to be lost are relatively low skill and low wage, those that would be gained are high-skill and high-wage ones.

13. Another argument is that while the international financial and trade institutions repeatedly push for "open borders" for goods and services and investment, the same push for "open and free immigration" is lacking. Bhagwati (2003) recently proposed a World Migration Organization. There is no international pressure group for migration.

14. Equity outflows were notably substantial, jumping to US$244 billion in 2008, compared to US$190 billion in 2007 (World Bank 2009, 37).

15. Or consumers preferred not to spend but to save in anticipation of an increase in taxes in the future.

References

Acemoglu, Daron. 2003 "Labor- and Capital-Augmenting Technical Change." *Journal of the European Economic Association* 1 (1): 1–37.

Aitken, Brian, Ann Harrison, and Robert E. Lipsey. 1996. "Wages and Foreign Ownership: A Comparative Study of Mexico, Venezuela, and the United States." *Journal of International Economics* 40 (3/4): 345–71.

Autor, David. 2003. "Outsourcing at Will: The Contribution of Unjust Dismissal Doctrine to the Growth of Employment Outsourcing." *Journal of Labor Economics* 24 (1): 1–42.

Bernard, Andrew B., J. Bradford Jensen, and Robert Z. Lawrence. 1995. "Exporters, Jobs, and Wages in U.S. Manufacturing: 1976–1987." In *Brookings Papers on Economic Activity: Microeconomics*, 67-119. Washington, DC: Brookings Institution.

Bhagwati, Jagdish. 2003. "Borders beyond Control." *Foreign Affairs* 82 (1): 98–104.

Blinder, Alan S. 2006. "Offshoring: The Next Industrial Revolution?" *Foreign Affairs* 85 (2): 113–28.

Brown, Drusilla. 2010. "A Review of the Globalization Literature: Implications for Employment, Wages, and Labor Standards." In *Globalization, Wages, and the Quality of Jobs: Five Country Studies*, ed. Raymond Robertson, Drusilla Brown, Gaelle Le Borgne Pierre, and Maria Laura Sanchez-Puerta, 21–61. Washington, DC: World Bank.

Feenstra, Robert. 2007. "Globalization and Its Impact on Labour." Working Paper 44, Vienna Institute for Economic Studies, Vienna.

———. 2008. "Offshoring in the Global Economy." Ohlin Lecture, Stockholm School of Economics, Stockholm, September 17–18.

Feenstra, Robert, and Gordon Hanson. 1996. "Foreign Investment, Outsourcing and Relative Wages." In *The Political Economy of Trade Policy: Papers in Honor* of *Jagdish Bhagwati*, ed. Robert C. Feenstra, Gene M. Grossman, and Douglas A. Irwin, 89–127. Cambridge: MIT Press.

———. 2003. "Global Production and Inequality: A Survey of Trade and Wages." In *Handbook of International Trade*, ed. E. Kwan Choi and James Harrigan, 146–85. London: Blackwell Publishing.

Goldberg, P., and N. Pavcnik. 2005. "Trade Protection and Wages: Evidence from the Colombian Trade Reforms." *Journal of International Economics* 66 (1): 75–105.

Haltiwanger, J., S. Scarpetta, and H. Schweiger, H. 2010. "Cross Country Differences in Job Reallocation: The Role of Industry, Firm Size, and Regulations," Working paper 116, European Bank for Reconstruction and Development, London.

Harrison, Ann, and Gordon Hanson. 1999. "Who Gains from Trade Reform? Some Remaining Puzzles." *Journal of Development Economics* 59 (1): 125–54.

Hoekman, Bernard M., and L. Alan Winters. 2007. "Trade and Employment: Stylized Facts and Research Findings." In *Policy Matters: Economic and Social Policies to Sustain Equitable Development*, ed. José Antonio Ocampo, Jomo Kwame Sundaram, and Sarbuland Khan. New York: Zed Books.

International Labor Office (ILO). 2010. *Global Employment Trends 2010*. Geneva: ILO.

IMF (International Monetary Fund). 2008. *Globalization: A Brief Overview*, http://www.imf.org/external/np/exr/ib/2008/053008.htm.

Jensen, J. Bradford, and Lori Kletzer. 2008. "Fear and Offshoring: The Scope and Potential Impact of Imports and Exports of Services." Policy Brief PB08-1, Peterson Institute for International Economics, Washington, DC.

Krugman, Paul R. 2008. "Trade and Wages, Reconsidered." Brookings Panel on Economic Activity, http://www.princeton.edu/~pkrugman/pk-bpea-draft.pdf.

Levinsohn, James. 1999. "Employment Responses to International Liberalization in Chile." *Journal of International Economics* 47 (2): 321–44.

McMillan, Margaret, and Inigo Verduzco. 2010. "New Evidence on Trade and Employment." Cited in Ravindra A. Yatawara's World Bank blog, May 27, http://www.google.com/search?q=McMillan%2C+Margaret%2C+and+Inigo+Verduzco.+2010.+%E2%80%9CNew+Evidence+on+Trade+and+Employment&ie=utf-8&oe=utf-8&aq=t&rls=com.yahoo:en-US:official&client=firefox.

Melitz, Marc J. 2003. "The Impact of Trade on Intra-Industry Reallocations and Aggregate Industry Productivity." *Econometrica* 71 (6): 1695–1725.

OECD (Organisation for Economic Co-operation and Development). 2007. *OECD Employment Outlook, 2007*. Paris: OECD.

———. 2010a. *OECD Employment Outlook 2010*. Paris: OECD.

———. 2010b. "Seizing the Benefits of Trade for Employment and Growth," http://www.oecd.org/dataoecd/61/57/46353240.pdf.

Rama, Martin. 2003. "Globalization and the Labor Market." *World Bank Research Observer* 18 (2): 159–86.

Revenga, A. 1997. "Employment and Wage Effects of Trade Liberalization: The Case of Mexican Manufacturing." *Journal of Labor Economics* 15: s20–s43.

Şeker, Murat. 2009. "Foreign Exposure of Firms and Growth in Developing Countries." Working paper, May 2009, Enterprise Analysis Unit, World Bank, Washington, DC.

Van Biesebroeck, Johannes. 2005. "Firm Size Matters: Growth and Productivity Growth in African Manufacturing." *Economic Development and Cultural Change* 53 (3): 545–83.

Wacziarg, Romain, and Jessica Wallack. 2004. "Trade Liberalization and Intersectoral Labor Movements." *Journal of International Economics* 64 (2): 411–39.

World Bank. 2006. "The Gains from International Migration." In *Global Economic Prospects*, 25–55. Washington, DC: World Bank.

———. 2009. *Global Development Finance: Charting a Global Recovery; Volume 1: Review, Analysis, and Outlook.* Washington, DC: World Bank.

———. 2010. *Global Development Finance: External Debt of Developing Countries.* Washington, DC: World Bank.

WTO (World Trade Organization). 2008. "Distributional Consequences of Trade." In *World Trade Report: Trade in a Globalizing World.* Geneva: WTO.

Yi, K. M. 2003. "Can Vertical Specialization Explain the Growth of World Trade?" *Journal of Political Economy* 111 (1): 52–102.